HOPE FOR THE
WORLD

Titles in this series:

HOPE FOR THE
WORLD

THE CHRISTIAN VISION

Roland Chia

Series Editor: **David Smith**
Consulting Editor: **John Stott**

Inter-Varsity Press

langham
partnership
international

INTER-VARSITY PRESS
38 De Montfort Street, Leicester LE1 7GP, England
Email: ivp@ivp-editorial.co.uk
Website: www.ivpbooks.com

First published 2006

British Library Cataloguing-in-Publication Data
A catalogue record for this book is available from the British Library.

ISBN–10: 1–84474–121–4
ISBN–13: 978–1–84474–121–2

Set in Monotype Dante 10.5/13pt
Typeset in Great Britain by Servis Filmsetting Ltd, Manchester
Printed and bound in Great Britain by Bookmarque Ltd, Croydon, Surrey

Inter-Varsity Press is the publishing division of the Universities and Colleges
Christian Fellowship (formerly the Inter-Varsity Fellowship), a student
movement linking Christian Unions in universities and colleges throughout
Great Britain, and a member movement of the International
Evangelical Students. For more information about lovel and national activities
write to UCCF, 38 De Montfort Street, Leicester LE1 7GP, email us at
email@uccf.org.uk, or visit the UCCF website at www.uccf.org.uk.

Contents

SERIES PREFACE

This book is one of a series entitled *The Global Christian Library*, and is being published by a partnership between Langham Literature (incorporating the Evangelical Literature Trust) and Inter-Varsity Press. Langham Literature is a programme of the Langham Partnership International.

The vision for *The Global Christian Library* has arisen from the knowledge that during the twentieth century a dramatic shift in the Christian centre of gravity took place. There are now many more Christians in Africa, Asia and Latin America than there are in Europe and North America. Two major issues have resulted, both of which *The Global Christian Library* seeks to address.

First, the basic theological texts available to pastors, students and lay readers in the southern hemisphere have for too long been written by Western authors from a Western perspective. What is needed now is more books by non-Western writers that reflect their own cultures. In consequence, *The Global Christian Library* has an international authorship, and we thank God that he has raised up so many gifted writers from the developing world, whose resolve is to be both biblically faithful and contextually relevant.

Second, what is needed is that non-Western authors will write not only for non-Western readers, but for Western readers as well.

Indeed the adjective 'global' is intended to express our desire that biblical understanding will flow freely in all directions. Certainly we in the West need to listen to and learn from our sisters and brothers in other parts of the world. And the decay of many Western churches urgently needs an injection of non-Western Christian vitality. We pray that *The Global Christian Library* will open up channels of communication, in fulfilment of the apostle Paul's conviction that it is only *together with all the saints* that we will be able to grasp the dimensions of Christ's love (Ephesians 3:18).

Never before in the church's long and chequered history has this possibility been so close to realization. We hope and pray that *The Global Christian Library* may, in God's good providence, play a part in making it a reality in the twenty-first century.

John R. W. Stott
David W. Smith

Preface

This book would never have been written without the help of a number of people. First, I would like to thank the Revd Dr John Stott for his invitation to contribute this volume to *The Global Christian Library*. The vision of this series is to provide an opportunity for Christian theologians and thinkers in the non-Western world to participate in the ongoing conversation on the central themes of the Christian faith in a biblically responsible and contextually sensitive way. I trust that by the grace of God this series will make an important contribution to his global church.

Special thanks must also go to David Smith for his encouragement and editorial advice. I recall the many conversations I had with David, both via e-mail and face to face when he visited Singapore, about the issues I discuss in this book. I am certain that David's persistence and careful advice have made this a better book than what was originally conceived. Above all, I am deeply grateful for his friendship.

I would like to thank the principal and Board of Governors of Trinity Theological College for allowing me to go on sabbatical leave from July to December 2004. The more spacious days of the sabbatical have allowed me to complete a significant portion of the book. I am also indebted to my colleagues for their encouragement

and for making Trinity such a stimulating environment in which to
teach, think and write.

I must also thank Philip Duce and his colleagues at IVP for their
professionalism, thoroughness and encouragement.

Finally, I would like to thank my wife, Serene, whose patience,
encouragement and love have enabled me to persevere in this
project. In many ways Serene is the embodiment of the life of
hope this book attempts to describe. In her quiet unassuming way
Serene has been a source of encouragement and inspiration to me
all these years. I dedicate this book to her.

Roland Chia
Trinity Theological College
Pentecost 2005

I

HOPE IN ASIA

Introduction

This book is about the nature of Christian hope. Hope is essential to human life. Some have compared it with oxygen for the lungs: without oxygen, death occurs through suffocation; without hope, humanity plunges into despair and is overwhelmed by purposelessness and meaninglessness. Hope energizes human life and serves as the essential fuel that empowers humankind's intellectual and spiritual endeavours. Hope is no less essential for communities than it is for individuals. Politically, hope may be said to be the source of civic consciousness and behaviour because it makes the future of our society, city or country inviting. Without hope, each person will simply recoil to his or her private life and seal himself or herself off hermetically from society and the common life. On the other side of the spectrum, hopelessness may 'motivate' a kind of fanaticism that ruthlessly, if despairingly, tries to remove every obstacle that stands in the way of the future. Only with hope will there be forbearance, on which all good human life depends and on the basis of which civility is possible. Hope teaches patience and creates that temperament which enables us to listen and speak to those with whom we disagree. For in hope we know that in the end everything will work out and that we need not fear taking our time.[1] Hopelessness is a kind of death because it opens the door to fear, and fear weakens and immobilizes.

More than half a century ago, the great philosopher Gabriel Marcel wrote these words regarding the nature of hope: 'The truth is . . . there can be no hope except when the temptation to despair exists. Hope is the act by which this temptation is actively and victoriously overcome.'[2] These words imply that hope is never abstract but always emerges from a specific historical and cultural context. The context from which I write, South-East Asia, now contains more than 500 million people with diverse cultures and languages, despite their shared history. South-East Asia is also made up of numerous nations, some of which, like Thailand, have histories that stretch across more than a thousand years, while others, like Singapore, are only a few decades old. South-East Asia also represents a diversity of religions, from animism to more philosophically sophisticated religions, including, of course, Christianity. The region is also a rich cultural and intellectual ethos, as traditional cultures and ideas blend and clash with modern Western ones.

In his sobering account of the consequences of modernity, Anthony Giddens argues that modernity brings to the collective psyche a disconcerting sense of ambivalence and anxiety because it introduces such radical discontinuities and fragmentations to society. The sheer pace of change it brings about and the scope of these changes, as different areas of the globe are drawn together in a complex network of connections that brings with it the clashing waves of social and cultural transformation across the globe, are unprecedented in human history. Vast institutional changes result as older institutions are transformed into something different, and new social orders, such as the nation state, emerge.[3] Paradoxically, the clashing of civilizational and cultural waves in the tempestuous sea of modernity bring about a new kind of integration, one that has political, economic and cultural dimensions, and therefore also implications.

Thus, in the modern situation, where 'countless bits of the world conflict with other bits', to use the graphic language of Patricia Crone,[4] a new integration is fostered, not by traditional values and outlook, but by the new 'isms' – rationalism, pluralism, secularism, individualism and relativism. It is an integration based on the present and not on the past, for it is the tendency of the modern mindset to be preoccupied with the immediacy of the present, thus only worsening its own rootlessness and instability.

> Being fragmented, the industrial world is unstable. More precisely, it is kept fragmented because it wishes to be unstable, the expansion of cognitive, technological and economic boundaries being its aim . . . Far from being anchored in a tradition, the modern individual is likely to drift: he has to decide for himself where he is going.[5]

This dilemma, which characterizes Western societies so well, is not alien to societies in South-East Asia caught in the nexus of the old and the new, and any survey of hope in Asia must give due recognition to it. The sea change brought about by modernity, the new challenges that present themselves in the changing geopolitical situation, and long-standing issues and problems that flood the collective psyche of those in the region give shape to new fears, as well as new hopes.

Terrorism and peace

On 11 September 2001 (9/11), when the United States of America was struck by the worst act of terrorism in its history, the world entered a new phase, characterized by President Bush as a 'war against terror'. To be sure, terror is not new, and its seeds can be traced to the origin myths of most cultures and religions. Indeed, history is full of tyrants and conquerors and the terror they wield. But when the passenger planes flew into the twin towers in New

York and the Pentagon in Washington DC, killing thousands of innocent people, not only were the images of that act of terror permanently embedded in our minds; they, as most commentators and political leaders agree, changed our world forever.

With terrorism, we are confronted with a new kind of enemy, the kind that cannot be seen. On 12 October 2002, two exclusive Bali nightspots frequented by Australian and European clients were bombed by members of the region-wide clandestine radical Islamist group called Jemaah Islamiyah (JI), killing 202 people, mostly Australian. This attack, which proved to be the most devastating in the world since 9/11, came only ten months after a previous JI plot to blow up Western targets in Singapore in December 2001 was foiled. Terror has become our narrative in Asia.

Since these two seminal events, attention has been increasingly focused on South-East Asia as the 'second front' in the war against terrorism. This is especially because of the region's large Muslim population and the many thousands of islands in the Indonesian and Philippine archipelago that could provide hiding places for al-Qaeda operatives fleeing from Afghanistan. Furthermore, it is known that Osama bin Laden has made efforts to spread the influence of al-Qaeda in the region by developing networks in South-East Asia for over a decade. With the world's largest Muslim population, South-East Asia could provide al-Qaeda with an endless supply of jihadists that would help it to achieve its revolutionary objective of a pan-Islamic community.[6] In the Philippines, al-Qaeda has provided ideological indoctrination, training and funding for radical separatist rebel groups like the Moro Islamic Liberation Front (MILF) and the Abu Sayaf Group, although MILF has distanced itself from the latter after 9/11. Al-Qaeda has also penetrated JI, which is a regional organization with extensive networks extending from Southern Thailand to Australia, and that has infiltrated groups like Jemaah Salafiyah (southern Thailand) and Kumpulan Militan Malaysia.[7] And with the post-Suharto crisis in Indonesia, the region appears ripe for Muslim revolution.

The member countries of the Association of South-East Asian Nations (ASEAN) recognize it is in their own interest to fight al-Qaeda and its associate organizations, and have developed a unified strategy to do so. That strategy has at least five levels: the national level, the subregional level, the regional (ASEAN) level, the ASEAN Regional Forum (ARF) level, and the international level. In Indonesia, for example, the government issued two presidential decrees after the Bali bombing to facilitate investigations and detention, thereby strengthening its legal and administrative infrastructures for dealing with terrorism. At a regional level, Singapore and Malaysia have good intelligence cooperation with each other against the terrorist threat, and both countries are working closely with Indonesia and the Philippines, and with friendly powers like the US and Australia.[8] The most important vehicle for combating terrorism is the ASEAN Ministerial Meeting on Transnational Crime (AMMTC), which is headed by the ministers of Home Affairs and which forms the core of the ASEAN Counter-terrorism cooperation. At international levels, ASEAN has been working with the Financial Action Task Force (FATF) or the Asia-Pacific Group (APG) to deal with the complex issue of terrorist financing.

Regardless of the effectiveness or otherwise of these strategies to counter terrorism, what has become clear in the events of 9/11, and in many subsequent events, is that everyone is threatened and that no-one is safe anymore. With these attacks, the political has become personal and the personal, political – religion itself, as one theologian exclaims, is no longer just a 'private matter'. As theologian Jürgen Moltmann wrote in the aftermath of 9/11, 'There is no personal life any longer without danger. Personal life has no meaning without political engagement in the necessary resistance against public terror and death, as well as the no-less-necessary work of justice world-wide.'[9] The phrase 'apocalypse now' has been used to describe human-made catastrophes like the nuclear catastrophe and the ecological catastrophe. With this new form of violence, an apocalyptic terrorism has emerged. The modern–antimodern

apocalypses, however, have nothing to do with the biblical apocalyptic tradition, because the former have to do with the hopeless
self-annihilation of humans and the annihilation of living space on
earth, while the latter is full of hope. To quote Moltmann again:

> the biblical visions keep hope alive in God's faithfulness to the creation in
> the terrors of the end-time: 'The one who endures to the end will be
> saved' (Mt 10:22). 'When these things begin to take place, stand up and
> raise your heads, because your redemption is drawing near' (Lk 21:28).
> Prophetic hope is hope in action. Apocalyptic hope is hope in danger, a
> hope that is capable of suffering, a patient, enduring, and resistant hope.[10]

Social challenges

It is probably true to say that few other regions in the world have
such extremes of wealth and poverty as Asia in general, and South-
East Asia in particular. Countries in the region with large
agricultural sectors are generally poor, and those that opted for
insular state-run development after the Pacific War are doubly
poor, having severed themselves from the emerging global
economy.[11] When the region's economies are measured in terms
of the Gross National Product, the range is from Laos, with US$1.6
billion, to Indonesia, at US$138 billion. But when population is
brought into the equation, the range greatly increases. For
instance, Singapore, with a population of 4 million has a larger
economy than that of Malaysia, which has seven times the number
of people. With a population of more than 200 million, Indonesia's
economy is worth just 31% more than that of Singapore. Instead of
bringing benefits to the developing nations, globalization has exacerbated the inequalities and accentuated the extremes of wealth
and poverty between and within nations. To be sure, globalization
has brought instant prosperity to a few, but it has also marginalized
and excluded many. In his paper 'Asian Societies in the Age of
Globalisation' Professor Randolf David from the Philippines
points out that globalization has 'brought tremendous dislocation

in the lives of the poor and of indigenous communities. It has made the sufferings and misfortunes of its victims appear as if they were part of the natural order of things'.[12]

Sociologists have in recent years been describing the emergence of a new middle class, a new bourgeoisie in Asia. The West has welcomed this phenomenon because it constitutes new markets for Western products, from processed foods to computer software to educational services. These people are conceived as the new tourists, who will bring foreign exchange in difficult times, the new economic dynamizers of the twenty-first century who can revitalize the ailing world economy. Appropriately described as the 'new rich', these private entrepreneurs have created an enormous impact, particularly in countries like China and Vietnam, where economic power has long been embodied in the bureaucratic hierarchies of the state apparatus. However, they have an ambivalent relationship with the state. As Richard Robison and David Goodman put it:

> The new rich do not constitute a monolithic and homogeneous category,
> and cannot automatically be assumed to have a vested interest in
> subordinating the state to society and making accountable its officials.
> They are both new allies and new enemies for old power centres.[13]

Be that as it may, the fact remains that the majority of the people in Asia are poor, and most Asian countries belong to the so-called developing countries. The message presented in the 1980 gathering of the Christian Conference in Asia (CCA) that 'Asia is affected in a particularly acute fashion by the vast problem of poverty, one which afflicts indeed a large proportion of humanity throughout the entire world'[14] still holds true. In his 1968 study on the problem of poverty in Asia entitled *Asian Drama: An Inquiry into the Poverty of the Nations*,[15] Gunnar Myrdall argues persuasively that despite the varieties of cultures and background, poverty and inequality are the general phenomena in Asia. Not every programme that aims to bring nations to affluence has succeeded in eradicating poverty. The long era of colonialism during which the peoples of Asia were placed under Western Imperialism, and which, according to one analyst, caused the breakdown of the confidence and creativity of the Asian people, is often cited as one of the major causes of poverty. But, as A. A. Yewangoe has rightly argued:

> This is not to say, however, that the era of colonialism was the only producer of all these troubles, or that once this era passed, the people enjoyed an era of affluence, released from poverty. As has been pointed out before, the control of the economic life of the people is still in the hands of the few, the authorities and/or owners of huge capital. They then form a small elite among impoverished masses, enjoying life and ignoring justice, often in collaboration with the new form of Western and Japanese colonialism, through the power of capital.[16]

The problem of poverty is exacerbated by the huge debt many Asian countries owe Western institutions and other developing countries, an amount that rose to the staggering sum of US$3,000 billion in 1994. One of the many causes of this is the escalation of oil prices that resulted after the OPEC nations got together in the 1970s. The enormous inflow of wealth into Western banks that resulted from this was used to invest in developing-world governments, with the belief that they were excellent investments because governments do not go bankrupt. Huge amounts of money were therefore pushed in the direction of the developing world without much research regarding the soundness or otherwise of these investments. Consequently, Western governments and institutions provided loans for development projects that were unproductive, and when the world economy was hit by a recession in 1980–1, which forced interest rates up, many developing-world countries were left with the burden of a huge debt. The debt crisis not only presents a huge drain on their economies, but servicing them also makes them substantial contributors to the economy of the rich West.[17]

Another possible problem has to do with multinational corporations (MNCs) based in the West, which expand their operations internationally, usually in search of cheaper labour and resources. While it is true that MNCs have generally been welcomed in developing-world countries, especially in Asia, and while their presence has benefited host countries, MNCs can impact host countries negatively as well. For instance, MNCs, because they are profit oriented, show very little loyalty to host countries and often pursue profit at the expense of the people and land of the host countries. One example (perhaps the most common) is when an MNC uses prime agricultural land in a mainly agrarian economy to grow luxury goods for the Western consumers, while the indigenous poor in the host country do not even have enough land on which to grow food for their own consumption. MNCs can therefore exploit their host countries, and seem accountable to no-one except their profit-seeking shareholders. It is clear that in Asia, the problem of poverty cannot be separated from that of justice. In most cases, poverty results from the fact that the rich and the wealthy lack a sense of solidarity with the powerless and the poor, which often leads to the exploitation of the latter by the former.

Religious and secular hope

Any attempt to understand hope in Asia must give cognizance to the role of religions because, despite the growing influence of secularism, the people in Asia continue to be profoundly religious. Throughout this book, references are made to the ways in which the various religions in Asia understand life, death and the afterlife, and how they differ from the Christian vision. My purpose here is to sketch, in the broadest strokes, the way in which great religions like Buddhism and Hinduism offer their adherents hope in the face of suffering and uncertainty. The fact that these religions have a long and profound influence on Asian cultures cannot be emphasized enough. In many ways they serve as powerful, if subtle, forces that have shaped and will continue to shape the Asian

world-view. As Roman Catholic theologian Hans Küng has rightly
argued, religion cannot be seen as a purely theoretical affair. It is 'a
lived life, inscribed in the hearts of men and women, and hence for
all religious persons something that is supremely contemporary,
pulsing through every fibre of their everyday existence'.[18]

Most religions, including Christianity, develop their idea of hope
in the light of their conception of human suffering and evil. This
strategy is especially prominent in Buddhism, particularly with
reference to its key concepts, *dukkha* (suffering) and *nirvana* (extinction). In the Pali *Dhammacakkappavattana Sutta*, one of the holy
books recognized by Buddhists as scripture, the Buddha states:

> Birth is *dukkha*, decay is *dukkha*, disease is *dukkha*, death is *dukkha*, to be
> united with the unpleasant is *dukkha*, to be separated from the pleasant is
> *dukkha*, not to get what one desires is *dukkha*. In brief the five aggregates
> [*khandha*; Sanskrit: *skandha*] of attachment are *dukkha*.[19]

Although there has been some debate regarding the meaning of
dukkha, many scholars maintain that 'suffering' is an appropriate
translation. However, it is important to have a clear grasp of what
constitutes suffering in the Buddhist view. According to Buddhism,
anything impermanent and liable to become otherwise is *dukkha*.
Thus even happiness is *dukkha*, because happiness is liable to
change.[20]

According to the *Dhammacakkappavattana Sutta*, the origin of
suffering is craving (*trsnā*): 'It is craving which produces rebirth,
accompanied by passionate clinging, welcoming this and that
(life). It is craving for sensual pleasures, craving for existence,
craving for non-existence.'[21] Notice that it is not just craving for
sensory pleasures that produces suffering, but also craving for continued existence (eternal life), and even for non-existence. This
concept therefore refers to a deep-rooted form of grasping that is
the intrinsic trait of the unenlightened person from the time of his
or her birth. Craving leads to attachment, which is grouped into
four types by the Buddhist tradition: attachment to (1) the objects

of sense-desire, (2) views, (3) precepts and vows, and (4) the doctrine of the self. Notice also that it is not the *object* of the craving but the craving and attachment themselves that are the determinative factors. Because suffering has to do with the state of mind, it cannot be eliminated by physical disciplines like extreme asceticism, but only by the transformation of the mind. And this is achieved only by meditation.

If suffering is the result of craving, it follows that if all craving can be eradicated or put to an end, suffering will also cease. In the Buddhist tradition, the state of total release from suffering is called *nirvana*, which literally means 'extinguishing', as in 'extinguishing a flame'. Briefly stated, *nirvana* is the result of the permanent cessation of all suffering, which is brought about by the cessation of craving. *Nirvana* is therefore an occurrence or an event as a result of which all the forces that lead to suffering are extinguished. Some critics wrongly interpret Buddhism as nihilistic because they think that *nirvana* refers to the annihilation of the self. Achieving *nirvana* does not cause an individual to cease to exist; rather it brings that person into the state of absolute peace and entirely cuts him or her off from the world. A famous passage from the *Dhammacakkappavattana Sutta* describes this state thus:

> There is in monks a domain where there is no earth, no water, no fire, no wind, no sphere of infinite space, no sphere of nothingness, no sphere of infinite consciousness, no sphere of neither awareness nor non-awareness; there is not this world, there is not another world, there is no sun or moon. I do not call this coming or going, nor standing or lying, nor being reborn; it is without support, without occurrence, without object. Just this is the end of suffering.[22]

Williams points out that a distinction must be made between 'nirvana with remainder' and 'nirvana without remainder'.[23] According to him the *nirvana* that the Buddha attains in this life through the eradication of greed and delusion is referred to by the tradition as 'nirvana with remainder'. When an enlightened person like the Buddha dies, there will be no rebirth. That is to say, the psychophysical elements that make up this individual will cease and will not be replaced by further psychophysical elements. This is called 'nirvana without remainder'.

Like Buddhism, Hinduism also offers hope for adherents in the form of liberation from the cycle of birth, death and rebirth. It teaches that enlightened souls travel along the 'paths of the gods', eventually reaching their destination in the world of Brahman. Those who have achieved this, according to the tradition, have been liberated from the cycle of rebirth and have attained oneness with God. Those who lived morally mixed lives, however, travel the 'road of the fathers' after death, and undergo a complicated process of reincarnation into various forms of life in the world, including vegetation.[24] The kind of birth that awaits a person depends on the good works or 'karmic residue' that this person has performed or possesses. Good conduct would mean that he or she will attain a 'good womb', (e.g. that of a Brahmin, Kzatriya or Vaisya). But bad conduct would result in the attainment of a bad womb (e.g. that of a dog or a pig). For the entirely lawless, the tradition points to a third possible post-mortem eventuality – they are reborn as tiny creatures with no chance whatsoever of breaking the cycle.

Hinduism presents two different basic human attitudes in the struggle for salvation, which are often described as the way of the monkey and the way of the cat. The baby monkey, according to the tradition, is active from the start, clinging on to its mother and finding security in her. The cat, by contrast, is passive, always depending on its mother for protection from danger. Human beings are accordingly divided into two categories: some try to reach salvation by their own efforts, while others simply cry out for deliverance. The way of the monkey comprises asceticism, the way of action, while the way of the cat points to the way of the love of God.[25]

It is important to note that the notion of *karma-samsara* is very pervasive in Indian religions like Hinduism (*samsara* = 'change'), and that such a notion militates against the idea of human free will. Although Hinduism presents the idea of God's supervising the operation of *karma*, it has very little scope for the concept of God's providential guidance of history towards an ultimate goal. Although according to the 'monkey' and 'cat' schools, divine grace could be stimulated by human devotion, there is no conception of divine providence as set forth in the Judaeo-Christian tradition. As Brian Hebblethwaite explains, 'without denying the reality of God, Hinduism has tended to regard the consequences of human action as falling under the impersonal automatic operation of the law of *karma*'.[26]

Any discussion of hope in Asia must give due attention to the influence of communism, especially in China. To be sure, communism in China is an intricate blend of Marxist socialism and Chinese religious and philosophical culture, resulting in a distorted version of the secularized eschatology proposed by Marx. The main tenets of the communist ideology can be gleaned from the writings of Mao Zedong that were canonized during the rectification campaigns of 1942–4 as the orthodox ideology of the Chinese Communist Party. The canonical status of Mao's writings is clearly evident in the imperative issued by Lin Bao and others before the Cultural Revolution of 1964–5: 'study Chairman Mao's writings, follow his teachings, act according to his instructions'.[27] Thus although *Maoism* does not appear in Chinese, Western scholars use it to refer to the thought (*sixiang*) of Mao.

Mao Zedong joins Karl Marx and Ludwig Feuerbach in rejecting religion. The Chinese communist view of religion betrays the influences of these two philosophers:

> Religion is a social ideology, 'the fantastic reflection in men's minds of those external forces which control their daily life' . . . the fantastic interpretations by religion of natural phenomena, social phenomena, and especially of oppression and class exploitation, play the role of paralyzing the minds of working people, and disintegrating their combat will.[28]

Yet Mao puts so much faith in the masses to bring about a utopia that he in effect divinizes the latter. Thus, in 'The Chinese Revolution and the Chinese Communist Party', Mao could declare:

> Our Chinese people possess great intrinsic energy. The more profound the oppression, the greater the resistance; that which has accumulated for a long time will surely burst forth quickly. The great union of the Chinese people must be achieved. Gentlemen! We must exert ourselves – we must all advance with the utmost strength. Our golden age, our age of brilliance and splendour lies ahead![29]

This is also clearly seen in Mao's idiosyncratic reinterpretation of a classical Chinese fable (*Lie Zi*) during the Seventh National Congress to the Chinese Communist Party in June of 1945 to portray utopia: 'We must persevere and work unceasingly, and we, too, will touch God's heart.' The traditional interpretation of this fable, which champions hard work and perseverance, is thus blended with Mao's mythology that speaks of God. But the next sentence quickly clarifies what 'God' means: 'Our God (*Shangdi*) is none other than the masses of the Chinese people.'[30]

Mao maintains that the realization of the utopian vision of a Chinese socialist society and universal communist state depended on hard work and perseverance and not on the working out of historical forces. *Datong* (Great Harmony), according to Mao, is achieved by creating a new humanity, uniting the hearts of both the little people (*xiaoren*) and the superior people (*junzi*) in thought and in morality. Is Maoism, with its emphasis on the new humanity (the New China) a substitute religion, an anti-religion or a form of atheism? Paul Rule is probably right when he writes:

> Perhaps Maoism is a substitute-religion, deliberately usurping the traditional religious ground. The attempt to apply an ultimate criterion, that of transcendence, has revealed an aspect of transcendence but one

that is ambivalent and inconclusive. The New China is certainly overtly anti-religious in its policy toward traditional Chinese and foreign religions again, paradoxically, this very inability to tolerate rivals may be evidence of Maoism's ambitions to be the one, true faith of China. It leaves no room for rivals precisely because of its ambitions to occupy fully all spheres of human activity including that we call religion. If it is not a religion, it looks remarkably like one.[31]

The fabric of hope

Hope is by no means the exclusive preserve of religious people or the Christian community, but a universal phenomenon. As a reaction to the challenges and difficulties of life, hope exists at a pre-reflective level of human awareness and activity. Hope, as some theologians have rightly pointed out, belongs to the very essence of the human condition, and is the presupposition and motivation of everything we do. As an 'outlook and attitude that influences and shapes and colours all human experiences and activities',[32] hope is thus essential for human flourishing. In order to attain a proper understanding of hope, a distinction must be made between hope and optimism. Optimism is the naïve and blind acquiescence to the principle of human progress that ignores the ambiguities of our world and the ubiquity of pain, suffering and evil. Optimism refuses to acknowledge the vulnerability of the human enterprise, preferring to embrace a triumphalism that has lost touch with reality. Hope, in contrast, confronts the world as it is – it embraces a stark realism, struggles with the ambiguity of life and 'responds to it by taking up a particular posture of imagining new possibilities and other alternatives, inspired by the pulses of human experience'.[33]

Since the Enlightenment, the confusion of optimism with hope has resulted in the latter being defined in terms of progress, the upward movement of human civilization to its imminent state of perfection. This modern idea of hope is doubtless shaped by the exponential advances in science and technology witnessed from the last decades of the eighteenth century.[34] Philosophically, this idea of progress is given substance by German idealism, which provided its metaphysical and even theological basis. This is seen especially in the philosophy of Hegel, which postulates the development of human civilization as the unfolding of the divine spirit immanent in the human spirit. And, through the theories propounded by Lamarck and Darwin in the nineteenth century about the evolutionary nature of life, the philosophical concept of progress in idealism finds scientific endorsement. To think that these developments have little to do with Asia is to underestimate the influence of ideas and to fail to see that even though modernization and Westernization may be distinguished, they are not always easy to disentangle.

Hope in progress, however, is short-lived, for its decline in the twentieth century is as rapid as its rise in the nineteenth. Even at the end of the nineteenth century, the voices of doubt can be heard in some quarters. But it was in the first decades of the following century that the triumphalistic creed of progress begins to collapse and is replaced by pessimism and anxiety. To be sure, some like Frederic Harrison could continue to be upbeat about the twentieth century. 'We are on the threshold of a great time,' he could write, 'even if our time itself is not great . . . It is the age of great expectation and unwearied striving after better things.'[35] But such optimism is not shared by the majority who witness the creed of progress being contradicted again and again by atrocities and tragedies that scar the history of the new century. Tinder, with his usual eloquence and perceptiveness, describes the disappointments that dashed the hope defined by the secular myth of progress:

> When the twentieth century began, we were unprepared for the misfortunes and crimes of our age, and our disillusionment was more profound than it might otherwise have been. The hope we inherited was laid waste by trench warfare, by totalitarianism in major civilised nations, and by death camps.[36]

Christian hope is defined in terms of transcendence in the sense that true hope presses beyond what we can rationally comprehend and control. The Christian faith maintains that transcendence cannot be attained through the exertion of human powers. For transcendence to be known, as Glenn Tinder has so eloquently argued, transcendence must act. 'Transcendence must disclose itself, and call forth the openness in which its disclosures can be freely accepted.'[37] Without revelation, our attempts to grasp at transcendence are at best the confession of our ignorance. But the transcendent God has revealed himself in Jesus Christ, and by this revelation, he has shown himself to be profoundly and deeply personal. The hope of the Christian is not in an abstract idea like 'the idea of the Good' or the 'unmoved Mover'. Concepts like 'the Absolute' or 'being-in-itself' found in different strands of philosophy (Eastern as well as Western) are far removed from the personal God of the Bible. In his revelation, God has presented himself as a conversation-partner and invites those whom he has created in his image into a relationship of covenantal love and trust. For Christians, then, God is not just the *object* of hope but is its *basis*: we not only hope *for* God but *in* God.

As the ensuing pages will show, Christian hope is profoundly different from the unbridled optimism of secular 'hope' also because it is cruciform: it is founded upon and shaped by the preaching and praxis of Jesus Christ concerning the reign of God. Christian hope does not ignore the reality of pain and suffering, but confronts them in the light of the death and resurrection of Jesus Christ. It is through the paschal mystery of the death and resurrection of Christ that Christian hope understands pain, suffering and death. As Dermot Lane explains, 'Christian hope resides in the crucified Christ, acknowledging that this historical reality includes both darkness and light, tragedy and transformation, sadness and joy, death and resurrection.'[38] Furthermore, Christian hope embraces not only the future but also the present, not only other-worldly realities but this-worldly ones as well. In this way, Christian eschatology is profoundly related to the doctrine of creation: if

God truly is the Creator of this universe, if this cosmos is really God's sanctuary, then eschatology must include the cultivation of creation and humanity in this life as well as their transformation in eternity.

2

THE HOPE OF ISRAEL

The God who holds the future
We begin our study of eschatology by turning to the Old
Testament. Although some scholars maintain that eschatology
appears only in embryonic form in the Old Testament, the latter is
nonetheless shot through by the theme of hope. The hope of
Israel rests in Yahweh, the God of the covenant, who has rescued
her from slavery in Egypt. God reveals himself as almighty, just
and faithful when he delivers Israel from bondage and guides her
into the Promised Land. The Exodus event (Exodus 3:7–12)
becomes the paradigm of God's salvation for Israel and the
demonstration of his love and faithfulness. Furthermore,
Yahweh's triumph over the gods of the Egyptians makes it clear
that he alone is God, and that the eighty or so gods of Israel's
enemies are nothing but dumb and impotent idols. The plagues
that befell Egypt at the command of Yahweh are signs of
Yahweh's greatness and sovereignty. Indeed out of the seventy-
nine times that the word 'signs' appears in the Old Testament,
twenty-five refer to the plagues of Egypt. Signs point beyond
themselves to something much greater. In the case of the

Egyptian plagues, the signs point to the sovereignty of Yahweh. They are a mockery of the 'gods' and the religion of Egypt. Through these signs, 'the Egyptians will know that I am the LORD when I stretch out my hand against Egypt and bring the Israelites out of it' (Exodus 7:5; cf. 8:19; 9:14, 17–18, 20; 10:7). Writing about the significance of the plagues, James Hoffmeier states:

> The Hebrew expressions 'strong hand' and 'outstretched arm' in the Exodus narratives, it has been suggested, were deliberately employed for polemical purposes against the Egyptian concept of Pharaoh's powerful all-conquering arm . . . This proposal is supported by language in the Pentateuch that describes Yahweh's arm defeating that of Pharaoh, thus demonstrating the superiority of the God of the Hebrews over Pharaoh (cf. Ex. 15:6, 12, 16; Deut. 9:29; 26:8).[1]

It is from this experience of deliverance that Israel came to understand that Yahweh is the Creator and cosmic ruler of the universe. The opening chapters of Genesis present in poetic language a brilliant picture of God the Creator and his relationship with the created order. These chapters make clear that Yahweh is the originator of all there is. He created the world from his own initiative, and was not coerced by any external force. He created the world by his Word, and was not helped by anyone or any pre-existing substance. These chapters emphasize that Yahweh is *absolute* Creator: he created everything that was not God. The Genesis account also leaves no room for the notion of an independent universe with the resources and means to sustain itself. Thus, according to Israel's understanding, not only did Yahweh create the universe; he also sustains it. 'These eight specific commands', writes Derek Kidner, 'calling all things into being, leave no room for notions of the universe that is self-existent, or struggled for, or random, or a divine emanation.'[2] The universe was created not only according to the divine will but also according to the divine purpose. 'Let there be . . . and there was'. This schema shows that the universe came into existence through the intelligence, will and purpose of its Creator.

Isaiah, reflecting on the soteriological significance of the concept of creation announces triumphantly the sovereign power of God the Creator:

Do you not know?
  Have you not heard?
Has it not been told from the beginning?
  Have you not understood since the earth was founded?
He sits enthroned above the circle of the earth,
  and its people are like grasshoppers.
He stretches out the heavens like a canopy,
  and spreads them out like a tent to live in.
  (Isaiah 40:21–22)

This vision of Isaiah suggests that the sovereign Creator is also the supreme Lord of history. 'God the Creator and God the Lord of history, political units, and society are one and the same. His foundations shape the fabric of nations and societies as they do the heaven and the stars.'[3] Isaiah brings out the religious implication of the concept of creation. The God who creates continues to work among men in recreating and renewing their lives. He never gets weary, but empowers the weak and strengthens the needy. Thus, at the end of the chapter 40 Isaiah could declare:

Those who hope in the LORD
  will renew their strength.
They will soar on wings like eagles;
  they will run and not grow weary,
  they will walk and not be faint.
  (Isaiah 40:31)

The whole point here is that God's creative power is focused redemptively on Israel's distress.[4] Yahweh will help those who trust in him, ground their hope in him and yearn for his intervention. Yahweh will also oppose Israel's enemies with all his might because of his great love for his people (Isaiah 63:8–9). By his great acts,

> all mankind will know
>> that I, the LORD, am your Saviour,
>> your Redeemer, the Mighty One of Jacob.
>> (Isaiah 49:26)

Israel can entrust herself to Yahweh because he is powerful and faithful. The faithfulness of God is established in the heavens (Psalm 82:2, 5), the foundation of his throne is righteousness and justice (Psalm 89:14). God's grace and his faithfulness are inseparable, and the psalmist delights in proclaiming his grace in the morning and his faithfulness at night (Psalm 92:2). In the Old Testament, the words 'grace' and 'fidelity' occur together some twenty times. Yahweh is said to have shown his grace and truth to Abraham (Genesis 24:27). He is slow to anger, 'abounding in love and faithfulness' (Psalm 89:24). Grace and faithfulness are Yahweh's agents and messengers of salvation (Psalm 57:3), and, as Creator of the heavens and the earth, Yahweh preserves fidelity forever (Psalm 146:6). Yahweh is gracious and loving, for he extends his love to all who seek redemption and forgiveness of sins (Psalm 25:7). Yahweh is faithful in that he always keeps his promises:

> 'Though the mountains be shaken
>> and the hills be removed,
> yet my unfailing love for you will not be shaken
>> nor my covenant of peace be removed,'
>> says the LORD, who has compassion on you.
>> (Isaiah 54:10)

Yahweh is therefore contrasted with the idols of the nations surrounding Israel who have mouths, eyes and hands but are powerless and can do nothing to help those who foolishly trust in them (Psalm 115:1–8). As Creator and Saviour, Yahweh holds the future. He is the basis and ground of Israel's hope.

The kingdom of God

Israel's faith in Yahweh the Creator and Deliverer led to her conception of Yahweh as cosmic ruler. The actual phrase 'kingdom of God' does not appear in the Old Testament, except in one form, 'kingdom of the LORD' (1 Chronicles 28:5). But although the idea of the kingdom of God is fleshed out and given elaborate treatment only in the teaching of Jesus, it is a theme found throughout the Bible. In the Old Testament, the word 'kingdom' is sometimes used in relation to God. For example, 'your kingdom' occurs in Psalm 45:6, and 'his kingdom' in Psalms 103:19; 145:12; and in Daniel, we read of the 'God of heaven' setting up a 'kingdom' (Daniel 2:44). Although it is sometimes argued that the Old Testament idea of God as cosmic ruler is taken from the polytheistic nature myths among the people of the Ancient Near East monarchies, there are significant differences between them. For the Israelites, Yahweh alone is God. He has delivered his people from slavery in Egypt and led them into the Promised Land (Deuteronomy 6:20–24; 26:5–10; Joshua 24:2b–13). In the Old Testament, as we shall see, Yahweh is not only regarded as king over nature, but also as Lord over history. Unlike the tribal gods of the Ancient Near Eastern world, Yahweh's kingdom is universal, extending beyond Israel and embracing the whole world.

Isaiah begins one of the trial speeches with the declaration that Yahweh is the 'King of Israel'. Here Isaiah places the three predications concerning Yahweh side by side: Israel's king, her redeemer, and Yahweh of hosts. These predications show 'God on the one hand in his majesty and on the other in his will to save'.[5] The kingship of Yahweh over Israel shows that Yahweh has created his people (Isaiah 41:20; 43:15), and that he has chosen them to be his special possession. He has also given his people their land and the power to overcome its inhabitants (Psalms 10:16; 44:4; 47:3–4).

Although Yahweh's throne is in the heavens, it is also said to be located above the cherubim in the temple. Hezekiah's prayer (2 Kings 19:15) acknowledges Yahweh's reign over the whole earth, on the one hand, but locates his throne above the cherubim, on the other. This emphasis points to the immanence of Yahweh in the history of his people. Brueggemann explains: 'the prayer makes the most sweeping claims for Yahweh while drawing Yahweh close to the elemental needs of Jerusalem'.[6] As King of Israel, Yahweh is also said to rule from Mount Zion or Jerusalem (Psalms 48:2; 99:1–2; Jeremiah 8:19).

The divine kingship is profoundly related to the earthly kings who were appointed by Yahweh at the request of the people. Saul (1 Samuel 15:11, 35), David (1 Samuel 16:1) and Solomon (1 Kings 3:7; 2 Chronicles 1:8–11; Nehemiah 13:26) were appointed by God as kings over Israel at different periods of her history. They were not to rule the people in order to achieve their own ends. Rather they were God's instruments and were given the responsibility to rule Israel on God's behalf (2 Chronicles 9:8). Although the human king played an important role in the history of Israel, he was to serve as the representative of God to the people and of the people to God. The human king had to acknowledge the fact that he served Yahweh, who alone is the true King of Israel, his people. Thus in Psalm 5, King David could address Yahweh as King:

> Give ear to my words, O Lord,
>   consider my sighing.
> Listen to my cry for help,
>   my King and my God,
>   for to you I pray.
>   (Psalm 5:1–2)

This way of addressing God is of course not only the privilege of kings. It is the right way for every pious Israelite to address Yahweh (Psalms 44:4; 68:24; 74:12; 84:3; 145:1).

Although Israel saw Yahweh pre-eminently as their King, they also understood that Yahweh's kingship has a cosmic character. There are many references in the Old Testament to the cosmic and universal rule of Yahweh; for example: 'God is the King of all the earth' (Psalm 47:7). 'For the LORD is the great God, / the great King above all gods' (Psalm 95:3). 'Say among the nations: "The LORD reigns"' (Psalm 96:10). 'The LORD reigns, let the earth be glad; / let the distant shores rejoice' (Psalm 97:1). The throne upon which Yahweh is seated is in heaven (Psalm 103:19), he is surrounded by the heavenly hosts (1 Kings 22:19), and from his heavenly throne Yahweh watches over all the earth (Psalm 33:13–14). The psalmists declare that God is the eternal King (Psalm 145:13) whose reign is from everlasting to everlasting. The eternal kingship of God is celebrated in Psalm 74, which associates kingship with salvation. Hence, 'But you, O God, are my king from of old; / you bring salvation upon the earth' (74:12). 'Salvation' here has to do with 'deliverance'. Yahweh is King because he is the salvation worker, who brings deliverance to the inhabitants of the earth by defeating his foes (74:4–9); namely those cosmic powers that work for destruction. Yahweh is not only regarded as King of the universe because he is the deliverer, but also because he is the Creator:

> For the LORD is the great God,
>   the great King above all gods.
> In his hand are the depths of the earth,
>   and the mountain peaks belong to him.
> The sea is his, for he made it,
>   and his hands formed the dry land.
>   (Psalm 95:3–5)

The reign of Yahweh is characterized not only by power and glory (Psalm 145:11–12), but also by righteousness and truth (Psalms 96:13; 99:4). It is therefore fitting that Yahweh should judge the world (96:10). As the righteous King, Yahweh will judge

the world with equity. Yahweh's judgments 'sets things right':[7]
he will punish the wicked and grant help and protection for the
righteous (Deuteronomy 32:36; Job 35:14; Psalms 50:4; 135:14;
Daniel 7:22).

As we have seen, Israel understood the reign of God as eternal,
as lasting from everlasting to everlasting. Empirically, however,
Israel was aware of the fact that both in her own situation and in
the present world the reign of God is not always visible. Human
rebellion, sin and radical evil continue to challenge God's kingship.
But Israel envisions the absolute and universal reign of God in the
future. One day, Yahweh will reign from Zion and the nations of
the whole world will pay homage to him (Isaiah 24:23; Obadiah 21;
Micah 4:6–7; Zechariah 14:9–17). In God's future kingdom, justice
and righteousness will prevail and evil will be no more. Thus the
psalmist declares that 'righteousness and justice are the foundation of his [Yahweh's] throne' (Psalm 97:2). In exquisite poetic
language, Isaiah portrays the righteousness, peace and harmony
that will prevail in God's future kingdom:

Justice will dwell in the desert
    and righteousness live in the fertile field.
The fruit of righteousness will be peace;
    the effect of righteousness will be quietness and confidence
        for ever.
My people will live in peaceful dwelling-places,
    in secure homes,
    in undisturbed places of rest.
    (Isaiah 32:16–18)

Israel looks forward to the day when she will have the privilege of reigning with Yahweh in his kingdom (Daniel 7:18). Israel
associates her hopes with a coming king in the line of David, the
'messiah', and it is to this figure that we must now turn our
attention.

The Messiah

The powerful and complex term 'messiah' literally refers to someone who has been anointed with oil. The origin of the term remains unclear, although its development can be traced in the Old Testament. This honorific title is used in the Old Testament primarily for kings and prophets although it is also occasionally used to refer to the patriarchs (Psalm 105:15), the Servant of the Lord (Isaiah 61:1) and the cherub appointed for Israel's protection (Ezekiel 28:14). The designation 'the anointed one' probably originated in Israel from the anointing of the king. There are numerous references to this ritualistic anointing in the Old Testament. David was anointed as king over the house of Judah (2 Samuel 2:3–7) and later became king of Israel (2 Samuel 5:4 = 1 Chronicles 11:3; cf. Samuel 5:17 = 1 Chronicles 14:8). Upon the death of David, Solomon was anointed king by Zadok the priest and Nathan the prophet, at the command of David (1 Kings 1:34, 45). But the king was not simply anointed by the priest and the prophet. Nathan reminds David that it was Yahweh who anointed him king over Israel (2 Samuel 12:7).

This is also the case with Saul, who was anointed by Samuel the prophet. Through the instrumentality of the prophet, Saul was anointed prince over his people by Yahweh himself (1 Samuel 10:1; 15:1, 17). Priests and prophets were also anointed with oil. Moses received instruction to anoint Aaron as high priest (Exodus 29:7; cf. Leviticus 6:20; 8:12). Aaron's sons were also similarly anointed (Exodus 28:41; 30:30; 40:12, 15; Numbers 3:3). Leviticus 7:36 emphasizes that it was Yahweh who anointed Aaron and his sons. There are a number of passages in the Old Testament that refer to the anointing of prophets. Elijah was commanded to anoint Elisha as his successor in 1 Kings 19:16. In Isaiah 61:1, the prophet considers himself to be anointed by Yahweh's Spirit for the work at hand: 'The Spirit of the LORD is upon me, because he has anointed me to preach good news to the poor . . .' Here, the emphasis is not an anointing with oil but an anointing by the Spirit of the Lord.

There is a profound connection between the notion of the king as Yahweh's anointed one and that of the eschatological Messiah. To be sure, Israel's monotheistic faith rules out the practice, so common in ancient Near Eastern kingship ideologies, of deifying the king. But in the royal psalms (Psalms 2; 18; 20; 21; 45; 72; 101; 110; 132) several very extravagant statements and predicates are used of Yahweh's anointed king. In Psalm 2:7, the king is declared to be the 'Son of God'. But how is this term to be understood? Drawing from Martin Noth, Hans-Joachim Kraus explains that in the Old Testament, the king is not by *nature* the son of God. At his accession to the throne, the king was declared to be Yahweh's son by the 'definitive will of the God of Israel'.[8] The king is therefore God's son by *adoption*. As Yahweh's vice regent, the king ensures that the land is governed in an orderly and just way. Thus in Psalm 72:1–4 we read:

> Endow the king with your justice, O God,
>> the royal son with your righteousness.
> He will judge your people in righteousness,
>> your afflicted ones with justice.
> The mountains will bring prosperity to the people,
>> the hills the fruit of righteousness.
> He will defend the afflicted among the people
>> and save the children of the needy;
>> he will crush the oppressor.

The king will rule for ever (Psalm 21:4) and secure the blessing of God for the people (Psalm 72:1–4, 12–14). Writing about Psalm 72, Kraus maintains that although the traditional 'messianic interpretation' cannot be simply adopted, yet 'it is beyond doubt that Psalm 72 speaks about the king of salvation in a manner that provides an impulse for more intensive thought'.[9]

Such thought is further nurtured in a context in which allusions to the Messiah abound. The Immanuel prophecy in Isaiah 7:10–17 points to the coming of the Messiah (Matthew 1:23), although no consensus has been reached by biblical scholars. Be that as it may, the messianic expectation is fully developed in Isaiah 9:1–7. This so-called Christmas promise came when the territories mentioned in 9:1 were already part of the Assyrian province. It contains the promise of liberation (verses 2–5), which will coincide with the crowning of the new messianic king of the house of David (verses 6–7). The investiture and the conferring of the coronation titles point to the fact that the eternal messianic reign of this new king will be characterized by justice and peace:

> And he will be called
> > Wonderful Counsellor, Mighty God,
> > Everlasting Father, Prince of Peace.
> > (Isaiah 9:6)

The picture of the Messiah as the double of Yahweh can be gleaned from many passages in the Old Testament (Genesis 49:10; Isaiah 9:7; Micah 5:4; Zechariah 9:10). The Messiah is said to be the judge (Isaiah 11:3–5; Jeremiah 23:5) and the bringer of peace and prosperity (Isaiah 11:6–9; Jeremiah 23:6; Micah 5:4; Zechariah 9:9–10). The statements made about Yahweh (Zechariah 2:10ff.) are later applied to the Messiah-king (Zechariah 9:9–10). The expectations of Israel with respect to *actual* kings are later transferred to the *future* king who will succeed where past kings have failed. It was from this complex of ideas concerning the ideal king that the concept of the Messiah was formed and nurtured.

The Messiah represents the means by which Yahweh will establish his kingdom. Throughout the Old Testament, God has always employed agents to carry out his work of salvation. The prophet who proclaims the news of salvation that Yahweh will bring about identifies himself as the anointed one of God (Isaiah 61:1–3; Zechariah 2:9–13). The 'Servant of the LORD' (Isaiah 42:1–7; 49:1–9; 50:4–9; 52:12 – 53:12) as the messenger of God's salvation will himself usher in the new age (Isaiah 53; cf. Malachi 3:1). The question that must be asked is whether it is legitimate to conclude that this eschatological Messiah-King prophecy of the Old Testament found its fulfilment in the person of Jesus Christ. Some commentators maintain that the idea is appropriated differently by different interpretative communities. There is thus for them a plurality of meanings in any given text that result in what Martin Buber has called the 'infinite interpretability' of the biblical text. Thus one interpretative community has chosen to identify the Immanuel of Isaiah 7 with Jesus and the woman with the Virgin Mary (Matthew 1:23). For Rad, however, '[n]o special hermeneutic method is necessary to see the whole diversified movement of the Old Testament saving events, made up of God's promises and their fulfilments, as pointing to their future fulfilment in Jesus Christ. *This can be said quite categorically*.'[10] Even the vicarious suffering of the prophets of the Old Testament pre-figures that of Christ. Thus Rad could write:

> in the Gospels these utterances of suffering, especially those of Psalm 22, accompany Christ's path up to his death on the cross. In all four Gospels the descriptions of the passion are meant to show that these words of prayer about the abandonment of the righteous only reached fulfilment in the suffering of Christ. So completely has he stripped himself of his glory that he could enter straight away into these sufferers' words, so that they express their own suffering.[11]

The Day of the Lord

The nation of Israel believed that the Messiah-King will usher in 'the day of the LORD'. The original meaning of this phrase can be gleaned from the way in which 'day' is used in the cultures of the Ancient Near East. In Arabic, for instance, 'day' refers to the 'day of battle', and it is most probable that Israel also understood this term in this primary sense. In fact, in Isaiah 2, this term is used to designate the Lord's day of battle in which he will use the Assyrians as his instruments. But although the term was initially used in this restrictive way, it soon took on a wider meaning in Hebrew. The 'day of the LORD' gradually came to refer to a special time, a time that belongs to Yahweh, in which he will reveal himself and carry out his plans. The 'day of the LORD' soon became a term used to designate Yahweh's strange and wonderful work in the world. Through his work, Yahweh will humble the proud and raise the lowly. He will reveal himself as the Lord who is to be exalted above all else. Isaiah proclaimed:

> The LORD Almighty has a day in store
>> for all the proud and lofty,
>> for all that is exalted
>> (and they will be humbled) . . .
> the LORD alone will be exalted in that day . . .
>> (Isaiah 2:12, 17).

The Day of the Lord is therefore the day in which God will be revealed in all his fullness and his purposes will be fulfilled. Thus the Day of the Lord is the day of salvation for the people of God. It is a day of joy in which the nations of the whole world, and not just Israel alone, will recognize Yahweh as king. This expectation is clearly articulated by the psalmist:

> Say among the nations, 'The LORD reigns' . . .
> Let the heavens rejoice, let the earth be glad . . .
> He will judge the world in righteousness
>> and the peoples in his truth.
>> (Psalm 96:10–13)

The Day of the Lord will see the promises Yahweh has made to Israel come to pass (Isaiah 42:9; 44:24ff.; 45:18–19; 49:14ff.), and Yahweh will emerge victorious over the idols of the nations (Isaiah 41:21–29; 43:8–13; 45:18–25). The Day of the Lord will therefore be the day of unsurpassed joy and gladness, for it is the day of the salvation of God's people.

> That Jehovah should reign, and that he should come to earth as King, must, in spite of all the terrors that might attend his coming, bring to the

world a pervading gladness. For the falsehood and injustice that had
cursed the earth so long would disappear, and the longing of men, who
were ever, in words and sighs, crying, 'Show us the Father, and it
sufficeth us' should be satisfied. But it would be a day of satisfaction,
above all, to Israel, when he should plead her cause; for the day of
vengeance was in his heart, and the year of his redeemed was come.[12]

The Day of the Lord is not just a day of salvation; it is also a
day of judgment, especially for Israel's enemies. In his vision,
Obadiah proclaims this impending judgment to those who would
harm Israel:

> The day of the LORD is near
>   for all nations.
> As you have done [to Israel], it will be done to you;
>   your deeds will return upon your own head.
> Just as you drank on my holy hill,
>   so all the nations will drink continually;
> they will drink and drink
>   and be as if they had never been.
> But on Mount Zion will be deliverance;
>   it will be holy,
> and the house of Jacob
>   will possess its inheritance.
>   (Obadiah 15–17)

By these words, Obadiah elegantly and succinctly gives expression to the sense of poetic justice that pervades the writings of
the prophets: destroyers will be destroyed (Isaiah 33:1), devourers
will be devoured (Jeremiah 30:16) and plunderers will be plun-
dered (Habakkuk 2:8).[13] But Obadiah makes it clear that this is
the result of divine judgment, and not an impersonal and mech-
anistic retribution.

The Day of the Lord, however, is not a day of judgment just for
Israel's enemies; it is also judgment day for Israel. Amos, for

instance, filled the concept with a distinctive ethical content. The Day of the Lord to Amos will be a day of divine judgment in which the wrath of God will destroy his enemies. Divine wrath is described in graphic and horrifying language and will be made manifest through calamities like the plague of locusts and the devouring fire. Israel will not be spared: her wickedness and stubbornness, her unwillingness to repent, will eventually lead her to ruin (Amos 7:1–9). Amos therefore issues a clear and grave warning, not just to the surrounding nations, but also to Israel, God's chosen people, 'prepare to meet your God, O Israel' (Amos 4:12). Isaiah points out the fact that many belong to Israel only by race: their true loyalties are directed elsewhere. They have sought after the superstitious practices of the East and the idolatrous practices of the Philistines (Isaiah 2:6): they bowed 'down to the work of their hands' (Isaiah 2:8). Because her lifestyle is indistinguishable from that of the pagans, Israel is 'judged to have relived the experiences of the "sons of Adam" and thus to share the same degradation, humiliation, and eventual judgment'.[14] The double-sided character of the Day of the Lord is articulated clearly and uncompromisingly in the prophecy of Joel:

> And afterwards,
>
>   I will pour out my Spirit on all people . . .
>
> The sun will be turned to darkness
>
>   and the moon to blood
>
>   before the coming of the great and dreadful day of the LORD.
>
> And everyone who calls
>
>   on the name of the LORD will be saved . . .
>
>   (2:28–32)

The salvation of God was not exclusive only to Israel but is offered to every people, nation and tongue. This motif is found in Genesis. The alienation of the nations of humankind due to the fall (Genesis 11:1–9) was immediately followed by Yahweh's call to Abraham (12:1–3). A new nation will emerge from

Abraham, which will bring untold blessings to the nations now under a curse:

> I will bless those who bless you,
>   and whoever curses you I will curse;
> *and all the peoples on earth*
>   *will be blessed through you.*
>   (Genesis 12:3, my emphasis)

This motif is expanded further in the covenant words of Yahweh to Moses as the representative of Israel. 'Although the whole earth is mine, you will be for me a kingdom of priests and a holy nation' (Exodus 19:5–6). There is a profound connection here between the duty of the priest; namely the giving of the law and the cultic blessings with the vocation of Israel and her mission to the nations. The same motif is presented in the picture of the humble servant of Yahweh going out to the nations to bless the nations with his salvation. This blessing constitutes light and covenant, the opening of the eyes of the blind, and the release of captives (Isaiah 42:7; 49:9; cf. 61:1). In a word, through the ministry of the humble servant Israel, the nations of the earth will turn to Yahweh for salvation. God's promise to the nations will be fulfilled through his chosen people and by his anointed one, the Messiah.

The Day of the Lord will also be a day of restoration and transformation. Isaiah sees a vision of the new order, the new heavens and the new earth, in which there will be perfect harmony and where pain and sorrow will be for ever removed:

> Behold, I will create
>   new heavens and a new earth.
> The former things will not be remembered,
>   nor will they come to mind.
> But be glad and rejoice for ever
>   in what I will create,

for I will create Jerusalem to be a delight
   and its people a joy.
I will rejoice over Jerusalem
   and take delight in my people;
the sound of weeping and of crying
   will be heard in it no more.
   (Isaiah 65:17–19)

The new heavens and new earth will be inhabited by peace-
loving creatures (Isaiah 2:4), and both man and the animals will be
pacified and live peaceably with each other (Isaiah 11:6–9; Ezekiel
34:28). The river that will flow from the temple will nourish and
fructify the land, enabling its fertile soil to yield many trees and
plants (Isaiah 47:1–12). The kingdom will transform both nature
and the hearts of men (Ezekiel 11:19; 36:26). The law will be
written in human hearts (Jeremiah 31:33), justice and mercy will be
the new social order (Malachi 3:3–4), and inexplicable joy will
prevail in human hearts and in society.

The afterlife

Having examined the concept of the Day of the Lord and the
cosmic transformation that will take place on that day, we now
look at what the Old Testament has to say about the fate of individuals. Traditionally, the first aspect is called 'cosmic eschatology',
and the second, 'individual eschatology'. We begin by analysing
the attitude towards death, depicted in the Old Testament. Even a
cursory reading of the Old Testament gives the impression that the
writers of the Old Testament are not primarily concerned about
reflecting on death. Other themes like obedience, apostasy, justice
and worship pervade the pages of the Old Testament. The concern
of the writers has to do with the way in which Israel conducts her
affairs in the light of the covenant Yahweh has made with her. The
Old Testament sometimes gives the impression that death is met
with indifference, and that the Old Testament's preoccupation is

with life, not death. An old man who has lived a full life will be able to accept death without much anxiety. This is surely the case with Abraham, whose death Genesis reports in a matter-of-fact manner: 'Altogether, Abraham lived a hundred and seventy-five years. Then Abraham breathed his last and died at a good old age, an old man and full of years' (25:7–8).

Upon closer inspection, however, we do find records of different reactions and responses to death in the Old Testament. There are writers who accept death as an undeniable fact of life with quiet confidence, or, some might say, with pessimism. The writer of Ecclesiastes is one such author. The author's inquiring mind and colourful life lead him to reflect deeply on issues relating to life's meaning and goal. He concludes his investigations by stating quite plainly that he sees but one end for both man and beast, for the righteous and the wise as well as the foolish and the wicked. Death to him is the great equalizer because it reduces all creatures to dust. Death is the final and inescapable reality that invalidates all our achievements and nullifies existence itself. There are also records of those who have felt the cruel blows of death and who respond with grief and protestations. An example is David's response to the death of Jonathan (2 Samuel 1:25–26) and his lamentation over the death of his son, Absalom (2 Samuel 19:1). Furthermore, there are records of the opposition of death in the Old Testament, and these come either in the form of a deliberate action to prevent or ward off the death of an individual (e.g. Genesis 31:22) or a specific law against murder (e.g. Exodus 20:13).

Is there a theology of death in the Old Testament? Does the Old Testament relate death to sin? And does the Old Testament provide an answer to death in its concept of salvation? The early chapters of the book of Genesis make it clear that Israel did not accept death as a natural phenomenon but as a consequence of humanity's sinful rebellion against God their Creator. According to Genesis, human beings are created in the image of God, and for fellowship with their Creator. The image of God in which humans are created gives them freedom, which they subsequently abused. Rebellion against the God of life must mean that the human being who was initially created immortal should now be deprived of life. 'The rebellion which is sin denies the divine sonship of man and the weakness of the human creature, and thus deprives man of a redemptive life with God, without which real life is ended.'[15] The prophet Ezekiel expresses the unequivocal relationship between sin and death in lucid language when he asserts that 'The soul who sins is the one who will die' (Ezekiel 18:4). The Old Testament therefore teaches that sin is not a natural phenomenon but the result of rebellion and estrangement. But the Old Testament also emphasizes that death, although real, is not the all-decisive event, because Israel's faith is in Yahweh, who is more powerful than death, and whose power over death will be made manifest in the resurrection.

Before we turn to the Old Testament expectation of the resurrection, we need to examine what it has to say about those who have died. In the Old Testament, the dead go to Sheol, the abode of the dead located in the deepest part of the earth. This is a place of darkness and decay, a shadowy land in which there is blackness, gloom and ruin (Job 10:21–22; 26:6). All the dead, whatever their status in life, go to Sheol (Job 3:13–19; Ezekiel 32:18–32), which claims its victims without discrimination. In Sheol, people's deeds are no longer remembered, and their life experiences, joys, sorrows and accomplishments vanish forever and are forgotten (Ecclesiastes 9:4–6). Here, human praise and worship of God also ceases. This is brought out forcefully in the Psalms. In Psalm 88, the psalmist reflects on the cessation of all spiritual activities in Sheol:

> Do you show your wonders to the dead?
>> Do those who are dead rise up and praise you?
> Is your love declared in the grave,
>> your faithfulness in Destruction?
> Are your wonders known in the place of darkness,
>> or your righteous deeds in the land of oblivion?
>
> (Psalm 88:10–12)

'The rhetorical questions in these verses', writes Tate, 'present the realm of existence in the netherworld as without the wonderful deeds of Yahweh and without praise for him. Even the mighty among the dead are incapable, or unwilling, to rise and praise Yahweh.'[16] The Old Testament makes it clear that Sheol is the abode of the dead, and is not the place of punishment for the wicked. Job, for instance, asserts that both the righteous and the wicked descend into Sheol (Job 21:23–26).

Numerous references in the Old Testament signal Israel's hope that Yahweh will in the end deliver his people from Sheol. These passages are found particularly in the psalms:

> But God will redeem my life from the grave;
>   he will surely take me to himself.
>   (Psalm 49:15)

> Therefore my heart is glad and my tongue rejoices;
>   my body also will rest secure,
> because you will not abandon me to the grave,
>   nor will you let your Holy One see decay.
> You have made known to me the path of life;
>   you will fill me with joy in your presence,
>   with eternal pleasures at your right hand.
>   (Psalm 16:9–11)

It is this expectation of Yahweh's deliverance that paved the way for the concept of the resurrection. In at least one canonical book, the resurrection is mentioned against the backdrop of the eschatological expectation that Yahweh will deliver his people from the finality of death and the shadowy existence in Sheol:

> But your dead will live;
>   their bodies will rise.
> You who dwell in the dust,
>   wake up and shout for joy.

Your dew is like the dew of the morning;
  the earth will give birth to her dead.
  (Isaiah 26:19)

The clearest reference to personal resurrection comes at the end of the book of Daniel:

'Multitudes who sleep in the dust of the earth will awake: some to everlasting life, others to shame and everlasting contempt' (12:2).

The theme of hope is therefore found throughout the Old Testament. Israel's hope is established in Yahweh, the Creator and Redeemer, who has not only rescued her from slavery in Egypt and defeated the gods of the Egyptians, but will also rescue her from sin and death and bring her to the bright new day of salvation. It is upon the foundations of the hope of Israel that the eschatology of the New Testament is erected.

3

THE FOUNDATIONS OF CHRISTIAN HOPE

Jesus and the kingdom

The 'kingdom of God' is the central theme of the public proclamation of Jesus. In the Gospel of Mark, Jesus proclaims at his first public teaching, 'The kingdom of God is near' (1:15). What does Jesus mean by these words? To be sure, the concept of the kingdom of God has deep roots in apocalyptic and eschatological speculation. During the time of Jesus, the people of Israel expected the kingdom of God to be established by Israel's Messiah, a Davidic figure, who will establish a reign of peace in Israel as well as in the world. Jesus retains most of the traditional expectation and teaching regarding the kingdom of God. He declares that the coming reign of God will end the dominion of Satan. But Jesus goes further than traditional conceptions of the kingdom by announcing that the kingdom of God has already come and by correlating the presence of the kingdom with his own ministry. Also, when Jesus speaks of the kingdom of God, he does so in personal terms, in place of the nationalistic conceptions of Israel. For Jesus, the kingdom of God does not denote a political or geographical area, but a conceptual framework within which the divine reign is to be exercised. Thus, Jesus' concept of the kingdom of God points to all those who would acknowledge the kingship of God, and is not confined only to Israel and the Jews. 'Such personal reference was unparalleled in Jesus' day, and it pointed to a different type of kingdom – a familial, not a nationalistic, one.'[1]

The concept of the kingdom in Jesus' preaching is profoundly theocentric. This is seen very clearly in the prayer Jesus taught his disciples. The petition for the coming of the kingdom is placed between two other petitions, the one for the hallowing of the name of God and the one concerning obedience to his will (see Matthew 6:9–10). The coming of the kingdom therefore has to do with man's worship of God and his obedience to God's Word – the carrying out of the divine will, on earth as in heaven. It is imperative that the theocentric nature of the kingdom of God is emphasized. The kingdom has to do not with the achievement or ingenuity of man and his culture. Rather the coming of the kingdom is 'first of all the display of the divine glory, the re-assertion and maintenance of God's rights on earth in their full sense'.[2] This is seen in the thematic summary of Jesus' preaching presented in Mark (1:14–15). The preaching of Jesus can be said to be in two parts. The first is the announcement 'The time has come', and the second is the summons 'Repent and believe the good news.' From this, one can deduce the theocentric nature of the kingdom: 'The kingdom "comes" – it is not created. It is itself the subject of movement, not the culmination of our movement. We cannot bring it in, but must be ready for its dawning.'[3] The theocentric nature of the kingdom means that its coming is not dependent on the activity of human beings, but on the divine will and the divine act. Similarly, the kingdom of God cannot be seen as a society created or promoted by men – a conception the Social Gospel movement and Liberation Theology share – but as a reality made possible only by God. Furthermore, the kingdom of God should not be understood as the natural, immanent process of evolution by which the world achieves perfection.

The personal connotation of the kingdom of God I have been developing means that its coming cannot be conceived as an abstract idea, but as the coming of God himself. This is seen profoundly in the many parables about the kingdom found in the Gospels. There is always a central person in these parables – God or his Son acting in his name. This is evident in the parable of the man who sowed good seeds in his field (Matthew 13:24ff.); of the king who holds his servant accountable (Matthew 18:23ff.); of a certain householder who planted a vineyard (Matthew 21:33ff.), and such examples can easily be multiplied. As Ridderbos has observed, the central characters in these parables present analogies of God's being and act in relation to the coming of his kingdom.[4] What this means is that the kingdom of God must be understood as the salvation God brings to humans. In the Gospels, the phrases 'to enter the kingdom of God' and 'to enter life' are synonymous, and often alternate without change in meaning (cf. Mark 9:47, and verses 43, 45). The invitation into the kingdom of God is the offer of salvation. Salvation is of course offered unconditionally to all. Numerous parables – the lost coin, the lost sheep, the great feast – articulate this theological truth. But while the offer of salvation is made unconditionally, blessedness is based on the condition that one accepts the offer. Thus, although salvation is a pure gift, its appropriation depends on one's acceptance of that gift. Humanity's entry into the kingdom is made possible by God's grace (Mark 10:24–27). But the gate is narrow (Matthew 7:13-14), and those who would enter it must choose to do so. Many are indeed called, but few are chosen (Matthew 22:14–15).

The kingdom of God is profoundly related to the figure of the Son of Man. This is seen in the way in which Jesus' proclamation regarding the coming of the kingdom correlates with that of the coming of the Son of Man. The two can be said to be synonymous (Matthew 10:23; 16:18; Mark 9:1). In some texts, references are made to the 'kingdom of the Son of Man' (Matthew 13:41; 16:28), the 'Son of Man [sitting] on his glorious throne' (Matthew

19:28) and the Son of Man coming 'in glory' (Matthew 25:31). All these texts point to the fact that there is coalescence between the coming of the kingdom and the Son of Man. It is the Son of Man who will bring in the kingdom of God; it is he who will bring the divine judgment. The relationship between the Son of Man and the kingdom of God in Jesus' preaching demonstrates that it receives its orientation from the prophecy in Daniel 7:13ff. The Danielic prophecy regarding the Son of Man stresses that this figure cannot be seen simply as an ordinary man invested with a temporal or earthly dominion. Rather the 'Son of Man', who comes in the clouds of heaven, enjoys the dominion, kingship and glory that are imperishable, just as the kingdom of God that he inaugurates has a universal and transcendent character.

Jesus' preaching of the kingdom of God is at the same time proclamation about the Messiah. For Jesus, the Son of Man is none other than the Messiah, the Son of David. The expectation of the Messiah is therefore the expectation of the glorious eschatological kingdom of God. Jesus speaks of the coming (*parousia*) of the Messiah that will bring about the regeneration or restoration of all things (*palingenesis*). But when Jesus speaks about the Son of Man on the throne of glory, he also alludes to the fact that his disciples too shall sit on thrones and judge the twelve tribes of Israel (Luke 22:30). Thus the 'prophetic' as well as the 'apocalyptic' expectations of the Messiah are bound together in Jesus' preaching. As Ridderbos puts it:

> The Son of Man is none other than the Messiah, the Son of David. But, conversely, the Son of David is the Son of Man, he who has been invested with divine and universal authority. And the relation between Israel and the Messiah must be judged and understood in this light.[5]

In so far as Jesus is the Messiah, the coming of the kingdom announced by him coincides with his appearance. But if the kingdom is already present with the advent of the Son of Man, why is it also spoken of as a future reality? This is because the kingdom of God, which has already dawned upon human history with the first advent, awaits its consummation in the future. But when will the fullness of the kingdom take place? I shall attempt to answer this question in the next section.

The time of the kingdom

We turn now to Jesus' teaching about the coming of the kingdom of God. Did Jesus expect the kingdom to come in fullness during his own lifetime and that of his disciples? In his celebrated *The Mystery of the Kingdom of God*, first published in 1901, Albert Schweitzer argues that at the baptism of Jesus, the secret of his messianic calling was disclosed to him.[6] Jesus then went about proclaiming the message of the kingdom of God, expecting the dawn of the great messianic age to take place during his lifetime. Jesus saw himself as the successor of John the Baptist whose mission was not only to bring the eschatological message of the kingdom to his people, but also to usher in the divine kingdom. Jesus' preaching, however, did not yield much success, and the delay of the kingdom left him greatly disappointed. When John the Baptist, whom Jesus had thought was the reincarnation of Elijah was beheaded, he knew he also must sacrifice his life in the act of atonement for his disciples.[7] He entered boldly into Jerusalem, claimed to be the Messiah, was arrested by the Jewish authorities, was tried and found guilty of blasphemy and put to death. But nothing happened after his death.

In *The Quest for the Historical Jesus*, published five years later, Schweitzer argued a similar thesis. The preacher from Nazareth proclaimed the coming of the kingdom, expecting that this would take place during his lifetime. This expectation ironically drove him to death, when the kingdom he preached and antici-pated did not arrive. The story Schweitzer tells is well rehearsed by theologians and historians who write on the historical Jesus. The wheel Jesus wanted to set in motion did not turn. So he lunged himself upon it; and when the wheel did turn, it crushed him under it. 'The wheel rolls onward and the mangled body of the one immeasurably great Man, who was strong enough to think of himself as the spiritual ruler of mankind and to bend history to his purpose, is hanging upon it still. That is his victory and his reign.'[8]

Although Schweitzer's thesis is no longer taken seriously by many scholars, the issue it raises regarding the delay of the kingdom still generates much discussion. Three important passages from the Synoptic Gospels, particularly Matthew and Mark, seem to indicate that Jesus had expected the kingdom of God to come in its fullness during his lifetime. The first is Matthew 10:23, where Jesus warned his disciples about the coming persecution: 'When you are persecuted in one place, flee to another. I tell you the truth, you will not finish going through the cities of Israel before the Son of Man comes.' There are several possible interpretations of this passage. The most attractive is that this passage refers to the *parousia* taking place during the lifetime of Jesus' disciples. Before the disciples could complete evangelizing the Jewish cities, the *parousia* would occur, and the kingdom of God would come in all fullness. This view is theologically justifiable, but has been proved historically wrong.[9] Furthermore, Matthew also speaks of the mission to the Gentiles, which will take place before the end of the age (21:43; 24:14). According to Ladd, this passage urges the reader to look beyond the mission of the immediate disciples of Jesus to Israel to that of the church. Ladd therefore concludes that Matthew 10:23 'says no more than that the mission of Jesus' disciples to Israel will last until the coming of the Son of Man'.[10]

In the second difficult passage, Mark 9:1, Jesus is recorded to have spoken these words to his audience: 'I tell you the truth, some who are standing here will not taste death before they see the kingdom of God come with power.' The other Synoptic Gospels also report variations of this saying. In Matthew it is rendered as 'before they see the Son of man coming in his kingdom' (Matthew 16:28), and in Luke we find the simpler version, 'before they see the kingdom of God' (Luke 9:27). What did Jesus mean by these words? Was he predicting that the consummation of the kingdom would occur within the lifetime of his hearers? Again various interpretations have been forwarded.

Some scholars maintain that this saying is not derived from Jesus but from the early Christian (Marcan) community and serves as an attempt to explain the delay of the *parousia*. In other words, this saying is inserted to assure members of that community that some of them, who were contemporaries of Jesus, would live to see this prediction come to pass. Others maintain that the phrase 'the kingdom of God comes in power' does not refer to the final consummation of the kingdom, but rather to the manifestations of the kingdom's presence in the ministry of Jesus; for example, his exorcisms.[11] Perhaps the best way to understand this statement is to examine the context in which it appears. In Mark as well as in Matthew, this promise precedes the transfiguration, and is there- fore in some ways linked with it. William Lane argues that this arrangement 'indicates that Mark understood Jesus' statement to refer to this moment of transcendent glory conceived as an enthronement and an anticipation of the glory that is to come'.[12] This interpretation augurs well with a passage in 2 Peter in which the glory of the *parousia* is seen in the light of the glory mani- fested at the transfiguration of Christ (2 Peter 1:16–18).

The third saying is found in Jesus' Olivet Discourse in Mark 13. After providing a list of horrific events that will soon take place, Jesus in 13:30 says to his disciples, 'I tell you the truth, this gener- ation will certainly not pass away until all these things have happened.' Does Jesus imply by this statement that his contem- poraries will still be alive when the consummation of the kingdom occurs? To be sure, there is no alternative interpretation to the phrase 'this generation' – it designates the contemporaries of Jesus (see Matthew 8:12, 38; 9:19). By this phrase Jesus affirms that the prophecy articulated in the previous verses will be fulfilled during the lifetime of his hearers. The phrase 'all these things', however, does not refer to the culmination of the kingdom of God as some scholars have maintained, but rather to the events described from verse 2 to verse 30; namely the destruction of Jerusalem and the dismantling of the temple. Thus, Jesus was replying to the question raised by his disciples regarding the destruction of the temple, but he did not offer any speculation or indication regarding the consummation of the kingdom of God. I therefore cannot concur with Craig Evans who contends that by the phrase 'all these things' Jesus refers not only to the events leading up to the coming of the 'Son of man' but *includes* the latter event.[13]

It is important to note that many passages in the Gospels refer to the delay of the kingdom of God. In the context of Jesus' Olivet Discourse, Jesus maintains that the presence of 'wars and rumours of wars' is not an indication that the consummation of the kingdom is near or has already taken place. Thus, although these signs 'must come to pass', they 'do not indicate that the consummation is at hand'.[14] Jesus used another term, 'birth-pangs', to describe the fact that these signs do not signal the end, but only the beginning of the end. 'Birth pangs' is often used in the Old Testament to describe the judgment of God and his eschatological action (Isaiah 13:8; 26:17; Jeremiah 4:31; 6:24; 13:21; 22:23; 49:22; 50:33; Micah 4:9–10; Hosea 13:13). Furthermore, these crises are said to be merely 'the *beginning* of birth pangs', suggesting that the triumphant return of the 'Son of Man' may not take place in the near future but may be delayed. 'These things are the beginning of travail' and the parallel statement 'the end is not yet' (verse 7) are in fact delay-sayings, 'designed to prepare the people of God for facing a turbulent world with firm confidence and unwavering faith'.[15] The delay of the kingdom is also stressed in the warning Jesus gave his disciples in Luke 17:22: 'The time is coming when you will long to see one of the days of the Son of Man, but you will not see it.' Parables like the importuned widow (Luke 18:1–8), the ten virgins (Matthew 25:1–13) and the talents (Matthew 25:14–20) indicate that the *parousia* and the consummation of the kingdom will be delayed.

Paul and the future

We turn now to the writings of Paul to glean from them the eschatology of their author. Even a cursory reading of the epistles of the apostle Paul would leave one with no doubt that hope in the God and Father of Jesus Christ is their central theme. It is not just in Paul's extended discussion on the resurrection in 1 Corinthians or the *parousia* in 1 Thessalonians that this theme finds prominence, but also in every aspect of his discourse on Christian faith and life. For Paul, the Christian life must be understood and lived in the light of the blessed hope – 'the glorious appearing of our great God and Saviour, Jesus Christ' (Titus 2:13).

The Christocentric nature of Paul's vision of the Christian life implies its eschatological character. The interdependence between eschatology and Christology forms the central motif of Paul's preaching and is important for the understanding of both. This is seen in Paul's tireless exhortations to the church to be blameless and pure as she awaits the Day in which she will appear before her Lord, the Bride presented to the Bridegroom. In the light of this great and awesome Day, Paul exhorts his readers to put away all works of darkness and respond to God's call to be holy. Eschatology also informs what may broadly be termed a 'Pauline theodicy', the justification of the sovereign and loving God in the presence of suffering and evil. The present world of suffering and pain will, at the coming of Christ in glory, pass away, and believers who now suffer affliction and distress will eventually find rest (1 Thessalonians 1:6ff.). The promised future glory all believers will share will be immeasurably greater than the sufferings they now endure (Romans 5:18). This eschatological hope is based on the love of God in Christ for believers, a love so strong and steadfast that nothing can come in its way (Romans 8:28–39).

Pauline scholars debate the question whether Paul had expected the *parousia* to take place during his lifetime. Although we look in vain to find texts in the Pauline corpus that suggest its author had a definite time frame in mind relating to the consummation of the kingdom, several passages clearly indicate that Paul stressed its imminence. In Romans 13:11ff., Paul exhorts the Christians in Rome to wake up from their slumber because 'our salvation is nearer now than when we first believed', suggesting that Paul believed the end is at a not-too-distant future. Also suggestive of the fact that Paul expected the coming of Christ to be imminent is the phrase 'The Lord is near' ('at hand') in Philippians 4:5. The assertion that 'the time is short' in 1 Corinthians 7:29 likewise reinforces the view that Paul had indeed expected the consummation of the kingdom of God to take place soon, as does his contention that 'this world in its present form is passing away' (verse 31). None of these statements, however, directly supports the view that Paul expected the end to take place within his lifetime. The qualification that the time is 'short' (compressed) is no more precise and therefore does not say much more than the statement 'the Lord is at hand'. But, as Ridderbos has rightly argued, the shortness of time is the basis for the urgency found in the tone of the entire Pauline corpus.[16]

1 Corinthians 15:51 appears to be the only statement which may be taken as direct evidence that Paul expected the *parousia* to take place during his lifetime. There, Paul writes, 'Listen, I tell you a mystery: We will not all sleep, but we will all be changed.' The plural pronoun in this statement compels some interpreters to conclude that Paul expected the *parousia* to take place within his lifetime.[17] Furthermore, 1 Corinthians 15:51 is comparable to 1 Thessalonians 4:13–18 (especially verse 17), which expresses the same expectation. But, as Ridderbos argues, although these 'nearness' pronouncements do seem to indicate that Paul might have expected the *parousia* to take place during his lifetime, we should not conclude that he did not consider another possibility.[18] David Wenham is surely right when he argues that although Paul emphasized the imminence of the *parousia*, he was not too dogmatic about its timing.[19] Furthermore, there are a number of passages which seem to indicate that Paul expected the *parousia* to be delayed. Paul had the sense that the mission to the Gentiles

must be completed before the final salvation (Romans 11:24).[20] In his letter to the Christians at Thessalonica, Paul also speaks of the 'man of lawlessness' who will be revealed before the end comes. The context does suggest that Paul did not believe that this figure was already in existence during the time he was writing.[21] These passages seem to suggest that however imminent Paul may have thought the *parousia* to be, he had expected several important events to occur before Christ returns.

Paul's vision of the eschatological redemption is not confined only to human salvation but to the transformation and renewal of the whole cosmos. In 1 Corinthians 15, we find the earliest and the most elaborate defence of the bodily resurrection of the dead. This is Paul's eschatological vision of humanity and this vision is firmly established in the resurrection of Jesus Christ (1 Corinthians 15:12ff.). The profound relation between the resurrection of Christ and Paul's individual eschatology is expressed in his second letter to Timothy. 'This grace was given us in Christ Jesus before the beginning of time,' Paul writes, 'but it has now been revealed through the appearing of our Saviour, Christ Jesus, who has destroyed death and has brought life and immortality to light through the gospel' (2 Timothy 1:9–10). Paul further establishes the relationship between the salvation of human beings and the liberation of the cosmos, which is now subjected to futility and bondage (Romans 8:18–23). He alludes to Genesis 3:17–19 and 5:29, which describe the divine curse upon the earth because of Adam's transgression.[22] Creation is subjected to futility not by its own choice but 'by the will of the one who subjected it', referring to God. But the point of this passage is that, although the earth has come under the divine curse because of Adam's sin, God 'still gave it a hope of sharing in human redemption or liberation'.[23] Thus 'Paul's vision of God's saving purpose drives him beyond any idea of a merely personal or human redemption. What is at stake in all this is creation as a whole and the fulfillment of God's original intention in creating the cosmos.'[24]

Already and not yet

How does Paul understand the interim period between the first and the second advents? The answer to this question is found in the central thrust of the preaching of the apostle, for despite its anticipation of the coming kingdom, the message of the victory Christ has already secured reverberates throughout. There is clearly a perception in Paul's preaching that although the church awaits the coming in glory of the kingdom, the perfect is already present, albeit only in a provisional way. This, to be sure, is profoundly important for Paul, for it serves as the hermeneutical key that unlocks the meaning of life between the times, so to speak. It provides a theological perspective that guides his approach to the ambiguities of the present reality and the ambivalent character of the interim period. It directs his focus to the comprehensive motif of fulfilment,[25] and away from the 'problem of the delay of the parousia'. In the same vein, this perspective informs Paul's understanding of the significance of the assertion that the kingdom is 'at hand', where 'at hand' does not refer to the length of intervening period, but to the relationship between Christ and the future. Interpreted Christologically, the 'at hand' enables Paul to see the continuity between the present and the future, history and eschatology. Faith sees the present and the future as an inseparable unity, and prophetically takes them together in Christ in its glance.

Central to Paul's eschatology is the resurrection of Jesus Christ. As an eschatological event that took place in history and is removed from the eschatological consummation of the kingdom, the resurrection of Christ for Paul shows that the salvation of God is already available in the here and now. In the resurrection, Christ has already defeated the last enemy, death, and has made manifest the immortality that belongs to the new aeon (2 Timothy 1:10). In Christ, the brilliant light of the new age has already begun to shine in the darkness of this fractured world (2 Corinthians 4:6). It is thus this 'realized' and 'still-to-be-realized' redemptive work of God in Christ that constitutes Pauline eschatology. Paul's Christ-eschatology enables him to assert boldly that believers in faith

have already entered the new age, for to be 'in Christ' is to participate in the redemption achieved by Christ. By virtue of the death
and resurrection of Christ, the believer has already been delivered
from this present age (Galatians 1:4), has been rescued from the
rule of darkness, and transferred to the kingdom of Christ
(Colossians 1:13). This is because in his cross and resurrection,
Christ has already disarmed the principalities and the forces of
darkness (Colossians 2:14–15). 'In Christ' is therefore a term which
refers to an eschatological reality that has already dawned upon
believers, as the present tense in this assertion makes clear:
'Therefore, if anyone is in Christ, he is a new creation; the old has
gone, the new has come!' (2 Corinthians 5:17). In Christ, the
believer has already experienced death and resurrection (Romans
6:3–4), and is already exalted to heaven (Ephesians 2:6). Paul's
Christ-eschatology allows him to encompass all of reality, past,
present and future, in his vision. Further it enables him to take
cognizance of the fact that the eschatological consummation is
not just future – it has already begun to unfold in history.[26]

Yet for Paul, the eschatological salvation and the consummation of the kingdom of God are future events. He refuses to allow
enthusiasm and utopianism to take root in his understanding of
salvation.[27] Put differently, while Paul emphatically teaches that
the salvation of God has already dawned upon human history in
Christ, he strenuously avoids an over-realized eschatology. The
resurrection of Christ is the first and crucial sign of the presence
of God's salvific grace; but, as Paul tirelessly maintains throughout his writings, the fullness of God's salvation is still future, and
the Christian must await it in hope. Consequently, the Christian
lives between the aeons, between an age passing away, and a new
age already here but not yet in fullness. As life between the ages,
Christian existence is riddled with ambivalence and ambiguities,
although Paul repeatedly assures his readers that this should not
be a cause for bewilderment. What God has ordained *will* come to
pass – the old world *will* give way to the new, and the Day of the
Lord *will* dawn upon humankind (1 Thessalonians 5:2). Paul was

not a philosopher of history, but he sees the *telos* of creation in the new creation that will emerge on the Day when the *parousia* takes place and when God accomplishes his purpose by bringing creation to its preordained goal. His is a theocentric view of history.

For Paul, the faith of the Christian has a tension-filled character because, on the one hand, it stands over and against this current world dispensation, this yet-to-be-glorified reality, which it should never idealize. Yet, on the other hand, faith is at the same time the certainty that God has already accomplished his salvation in Christ, who by his death and resurrection has won the victory. The tension-filled character of the faith of the believer, which must hold in balance the 'already' and the 'not yet', is portrayed repeatedly and variously in Paul's epistles. For him, as we have seen, the new creation has already begun, and yet, it is also the case that believers are living in this present aeon, in a world fractured by sin, evil and death (Romans 8:18; 11:5; 12:2). Expressions like 'the end of the ages' or the 'last days' have two meanings. On the one hand, they refer to the church in history, while, on the other, they are used to refer to the period upon which the church will enter in the future (2 Timothy 3:1). Christians are snatched by Christ from the present evil age (Galatians 1:14), and yet it is in this present age that Christians must live exemplary and godly lives (Titus 2:12). Examples of such duality and polarizations can be multiplied with ease. It would be tempting to conclude from this that Paul is primarily a 'theologian who thought in terms of aeons', that he develops his thinking about Christian existence within the schema provided by the idea of the ages. But such approaches to Paul's eschatology must be resisted for reasons I have delineated earlier; namely that Paul's is a Christ-eschatology; that is, his reflection on eschatology is based on Christ, and not on some abstract schema. Ridderbos is right to observe:

> Here is the reason why this eschatology is ambivalent and fits into no single schema, and why he [Paul] can employ the eschatological categories at one time in a present, and at another time in a future sense,

apparently without concerning himself about the 'unsystematic' character of it. The revelation of Jesus Christ as the Messiah promised by God to Israel determines and creates Paul's historical consciousness and eschatological thought, and not the reverse. Who Christ is and what he does, what the relationship is between the time of salvation that has been entered upon with him and the future still to be expected, all this is not determined by eschatological-theological presuppositions, but is only gathered by the apostle from the unexpected and overwhelming manner in which God in Jesus Christ has given and will yet give the fulfillment of the redemptive promise.[28]

4

THE LAST ENEMY

My survey of the biblical material in the last two chapters has demonstrated that the Bible is permeated with the theme of hope. It is important that this fact is emphasized anew today because for too long eschatology has been related as 'the last things', an appendix to Christian dogmatics. As theologians like Jürgen Moltmann and Wolfhart Pannenberg have argued so powerfully, the Christian faith must be understood eschatologically. My survey of the biblical material has also shown that central to the Bible's understanding of hope is the work of God in Christ. Eschatology and Christology are profoundly related to one another, and any attempt to separate the two will result in a distorted understanding of the nature of hope. In a similar vein, eschatology must be seen in relation to the other aspects of the Christian faith, and cannot be viewed in isolation from them. To some extent, both Catholic and Protestant dogmatics have been guilty of this erroneous approach. Commenting on seventeenth-century Protestant dogmatics, Pannenberg observed that its eschatology had 'little to do with its understanding of Christ and the atonement, the sacramental life of the Church and the dialectic of Christian existence –

all this was understood independent of eschatology'.[1] In the following chapters, we turn our attention to the *eschata*, the four last things: death, judgment, heaven and hell. It is interesting to note that in the traditional list, the resurrection, so central to the Christian faith, is left out. In the succeeding chapters, therefore, I shall go beyond the 'four last things' as traditionally conceived, to present a comprehensive account of the hope of the church as delineated in Scripture.

Theology of death
The reality of death

We begin by delineating a theology of death. Death is an undeniable phenomenon, and every culture has something of a mythology or metaphysics of death. In Chinese culture, for instance, such a varied complex of beliefs regarding death and the dead exists that it is impossible to describe precisely popular beliefs about heaven, hell, the afterlife and the supernatural.[2] That the Chinese believe that death is not the absolute terminus of life, and that there is life after death, is evidenced in the ubiquitous family altar in the home of a Chinese family. The family altar serves as a small shrine, and is usually given pride of place in the main room of the house. On it is placed a number of deities – according to the taste of the family in question – and an ancestral tablet containing the names of the ancestors of the family, including those who have recently died. Offerings and prayers are made to the deities and ancestors alike. The Chinese believe that the dead are able to help the living, so prayers are offered to one's ancestors in order to attain blessings from them. In their search for an elixir that would prolong life, the Chinese, especially the Taoists, reveal another aspect of their attitude towards death.[3] Here, immortality is understood as longevity, where death itself is cheated. Similarly, different theories about death and immortality can be found in Greek philosophy and culture. These range from a naturalistic approach, in which death is seen simply as the absolute termination of life (Empedocles) to an elaborate theory of the immortality of the soul (Plato).

Human beings are anxious about their deaths for two reasons. The first has to do with the knowledge that death is inevitable. This situation is made more complex because among sensate creatures, only human beings seem to have an awareness of death.[4] We live our lives knowing that death is irrevocable, unconditioned and ultimate, and we conduct our affairs in the light of this knowledge, whether we realize it or not. Furthermore, experience tells us that death not only strikes us in old age; it can strike the very young, and those in the middle of life and at the height of their powers, with so much to look forward to. Death is not something that *may* happen to each of us, but something that is *bound* to happen.[5] Many things that appear to be inevitable are in fact only so conditionally, because the conditions are placed in our hands. This is not the case with death, which is not in our hands, but in God's.

Secondly, although we know that we shall die one day, we do not know when this will happen and how. There is a sense in which we constantly live our lives in the shadow of death. Existentialist philosophers respond to this anxiety by urging us to face up to the reality of death, to accept it as inevitable.[6] The unwillingness or failure to do this, they maintain, results in 'inauthentic existence'. Thus, in order to live one's life properly and fruitfully, one must accept the certainty of death. Existentialists maintain that death is merely the end of the process, the final stage of life, and we are wise if we accept it. This approach is inimical to that of the Christian faith, as we shall see. For Christians, death is not part of the process of life, even if it signals life's end. Death, for the Christian, is a contradiction to life, an antithesis to the divine purpose.

The nature of death

How are we to understand death? What is its nature? At one level – the clinical and biological – death is understood simply as the cessation of life. The standard definition of clinical death is based

on one main criterion, namely, the 'irreversible loss of function of
the organism as a whole'.[7] Here death is defined in purely biological terms: the absence of pulse or heartbeat, the lack of eye reflex,
the absence of respiration and so on. But from the standpoint of
philosophy, such a definition is inadequate because it fails to take
into consideration the fact that death can be properly understood
only with reference to life itself. If life is our participation in the
process of our environment, death must be understood as the
final and irreversible cessation of that participation. Of course
each of us participates in life differently. The participation
expressed by a scientist in the prime of her life and at the height of
her career is very different from that of a young man in an inten-
sive-care unit fighting a terminal disease. But regardless of what
one's participation in life may entail, death is defined, according to
this approach, as its irreversible cessation. As Hans Schwarz has
put it, 'Understanding death from the view of life as this active
participation could free us from a strictly biological understanding
of death as the irreversible end of certain processes.'[8] But even
such an approach would fail to address the ambiguity and terror of
death. The term 'euthanasia' (which in Greek means 'good death')
is therefore a serious misnomer, since there is no such thing as a
good death.

From the standpoint of theology, death cannot be understood
purely as the cessation of life in the physical body. There are,
however, a number of Scripture passages that describe death in
this way. In Matthew 10:28, Jesus contrasts physical death with the
death of the body *and* the soul when he says, 'Do not be afraid of
those who kill the body but cannot kill the soul. Rather, be afraid
of the One who can destroy both soul and body in hell' (see also
Luke 12:4–5). But, in addition to physical death, Scripture also
speaks of spiritual and eternal death. Spiritual death has to do
with the separation of the human being from God, who is the
source of life. Eternal death refers to the final and irrevocable state
of this separation. Paul was referring to spiritual deadness when
he wrote to the Ephesians, 'As for you, you were dead in your

transgressions and sins, in which you used to live when you followed the ways of the world and of the ruler of the kingdom of the air, the spirit who is now at work in those who are disobedient' (Ephesians 2:1–2). In the book of Revelation, eternal death is described as the 'second death', the final state of those who continue to reject God. 'But the cowardly, the unbelieving, the vile, the murderers, the sexually immoral, those who practise magic arts, the idolaters and all liars – their place will be in the fiery lake of burning sulphur. This is the second death' (Revelation 21:8). These passages not only show that death cannot simply be understood as the cessation of life, but also that death is unnatural, for death robs us of the gift of life that comes from God.

Sin and death

There is a great deal of debate today in some theological circles about whether human beings are born mortal or immortal. Some theologians regard physical death as the natural end of finite creatures, not the consequence of sin. According to these theologians, when Paul speaks of death as the wages of sin, he was referring to 'the fear of death' and not physical death as such. Because sinful human beings are estranged from their Creator, they refuse to accept death as a natural end of life. As we survey the pages of the Old and New Testaments, we notice a number of passages that refer directly to the relationship between sin and spiritual death. An example of such a text is Ezekiel 18:4, 20, which categorically states that 'the soul that sins shall die'. That this text refers to spiritual death is substantiated by the assertion which follows immediately, that the repentant shall live (verses 21–22). The same can be said of Romans 6:23, where Paul maintains, again quite categorically, that 'the wages of sin is death'. This interpretation is established by the fact that this passage contrasts the death that is the consequence of sin with eternal life.

It is in Paul's defence of the resurrection that the relationship between sin and *physical* death is more explicitly articulated. In his discussion of the resurrection, Paul presents the relationship between sin and death thus: 'For since death came through a man, the resurrection of the dead comes also through a man' (1 Corinthians 15:21). This verse therefore shows quite clearly that physical death is the result of human sin, and that death is not the original intention of God for humankind. That is to say, if human beings did not sin, death would not have come into the world. The fact that death is inimical to the purpose of God is also brought out by the Pauline statement that death is an enemy (1 Corinthians 15:26). As something foreign and hostile, physical death is depicted as that which opposes God, an enemy to be conquered.

For Paul, the resurrection of Christ signals clearly the complete and irrevocable victory of God over the last enemy, death. 'Where, O death, is your victory? Where, O death, is your sting? The sting of death is sin, and the power of sin is the law. But thanks be to God! He gives us the victory through our Lord Jesus Christ' (1 Corinthians 15:55–56). For Paul, therefore, death cannot be seen as the necessary consequence of finitude and as part of life. Death is an enemy that has been conquered by the victorious resurrection of Christ. But if in the resurrection, Christ has indeed conquered death, why do believers still die? To answer this question we must recall our earlier discussion about the kingdom of God. We saw that the kingdom inaugurated by Christ is not yet here in all its fullness but must await its consummation at the *parousia*. In the light of this, Paul maintains that although God in Christ has vanquished death, it would only be fully eradicated when the kingdom of God comes in fullness.

In the meantime, believers will still die but their entire attitude towards death is radically changed, because death no longer poses a threat to them. For the unbeliever, death is a curse: it is not merely an end to earthly life but is also eternal separation from God. For the believer, however, the curse is gone, death has become a vanquished enemy now forced to submit to the will of God. That is why Paul could even say that for him death is desirable: 'For me, to live is Christ and to die is gain. If I am to go on living in the body, this will mean fruitful labour for me. Yet what shall I choose? I do not know! I am torn between the two: I desire to depart and be with Christ, which is better by far . . .' (Philippians 1:21–23). The believer can therefore face the prospect of death without fear because she knows that the effect of death is not final, for death is a vanquished enemy.

The intermediate state

Where do the dead go? This question presupposes that physical death is not the termination of existence, and that something survives it. The Chinese culture and its syncretistic religions have much to say about the dead. As the popular folk ceremonies of death and burial clearly show, the spirit (or soul?) of the departed goes to another world. Relatives of the deceased will help him in his journey to this other world by rituals so elaborate and diverse that it is difficult to develop a consistent picture. The Chinese do not really have an idea of the soul. Taoism avoids the issue altogether, and Buddhism upholds reincarnation, a belief in no way universal among the Chinese. Like African cultures, the Chinese believe that their departed relatives are somehow still 'with' those who are alive. A colleague of mine has compared this with the Christian concept of the 'communion of saints'. In any case, according to the Chinese, when second uncle dies, his spirit is still with the family. He still retains his personality as second uncle as far as the family is concerned. Some Chinese believe that sickness, poverty and misfortune are caused by the unhappy spirits of the dead. The living members of the society have a continuing obligation to appease them, or risk being besieged by these restless and trouble-making spirits.

Philosophically, the Chinese uphold a body–spirit dualism. Modern wholistic anthropology, which postulates the unitary view of a human being, rejects the dualism that speaks of a body *and* a soul, as if these are different and fairly autonomous entities (substances). Before we get to this issue, I shall examine some proposals that have been forwarded in the history of theology regarding the intermediate state between death and resurrection. We shall return to the question of the soul after this brief survey.

Theories regarding the intermediate state
Soul sleep

The idea of soul sleep has enjoyed considerable popularity in some Christian circles. This idea can be traced to the great Reformer Martin Luther who used the metaphor to describe the state between death and resurrection. During this period, the soul enters into a state of repose, and at the resurrection the human being, both body and soul, will be raised. 'For just as a man who falls sleep and sleeps soundly until the morning does not know what has happened to him when he wakes up, so we shall suddenly rise on the Last Day; and we shall know neither what death has been like or how we have come through it.'[9] Although Lutheran orthodoxy after Luther did not embrace the Reformer's teaching in this aspect, many others, notably the Anabaptists and Socinians, did. Today, Seventh-Day Adventists and the Jehovah's Witnesses hold this view, although for the Adventists, the term 'soul sleep' is something of a misnomer. As Anthony Hoekema has pointed out, the Adventists' position may be more accurately described as 'soul-extinction', since they believe that nothing survives death.[10] Be that as it may, soul sleep is attractive for the simple reason that the Bible itself uses this metaphor to describe death (see, for instance, Acts 7:60; 1 Corinthians 15:6, 18, 20, 51).

The theory of soul sleep, however, is not without problems. The primary problem has to do with the way in which the metaphor 'sleep' is understood in the New Testament itself. As some interpreters maintain, this metaphor, although frequently used to depict death, does not in fact describe the state of the dead. In other words, the problem is chiefly a hermeneutical one: that which serves as a euphemism for the cessation of life is wrongly taken as a literal description of the state of the soul after death. If the first problem has to do with hermeneutics, the second is associated with the anthropology the concept of 'soul sleep' requires. As mentioned earlier, the dualistic anthropology, which postulates that the human being is made up of two substances, body and soul, has fallen out of favour today. The unitary view of the human being, which has gained wide acceptance, in the main militates against the essential presupposition of the doctrine of soul sleep; namely that something (the soul) survives physical death. This, above all others, can be said to be the primary reason why this doctrine, once quite commonly held, has now fallen into disfavour.

Instantaneous resurrection

In recent times, a novel and attractive approach, namely the theory of instantaneous resurrection, has been forwarded and has attracted many Roman Catholic as well as Protestant theologians. Writing in 1955, W. D. Davies, in *Paul and Rabbinic Judaism*, presents a version of this theory by arguing that Paul's understanding of the resurrection changed. A simple comparison between 1 Corinthians 15 and 2 Corinthians 5 shows this. According to Davies, in 1 Corinthians 15, Paul embraced the rabbinic concept, which postulates the resurrection as a future event during which the soul, disembodied at death, will receive a new body. This view, however, underwent significant changes in 2 Corinthians 5, where Paul argues that believers, having died and risen with Christ, are already transformed and will receive their new bodies immediately upon physical death:

> [The dead will], on the contrary, be embodied, and there is no room in Paul's theology for an intermediate state of the dead. It agrees with this that Paul in later passages of his Epistles speaks not of the resurrection of Christians but of their revelation. In Rom 8:19 we read: 'The earnest longing of creation waiteth for the revelation of the sons of God'; and in Col 3:4 we read: 'When Christ who is our life shall be revealed then shall ye also be revealed with him in glory.' There is no need to resurrect those who have already died and risen with Christ and received their heavenly body, but they may be revealed. The final consummation would merely

be the manifestation of that which is already existent but 'hidden' in the eternal order. [11]

The attractiveness of this theory lies in the fact that it comports with a unitary view of man, and altogether eliminates the need to speculate about the intermediate state. But, as evangelical theologian Millard Erickson is right to point out, the problem lies in Davies' interpretation of Paul, which sees as contradictory that which is meant to be complementary.[12] Although Davies suggests that the two passages in the Corinthian correspondences should be understood as providing two very different views of the resurrection at different stages in the thought of Paul, he offers little basis for putting forward such an interpretation. Davies also fails to appreciate the relationship between the resurrection and the *parousia*, which Paul emphasizes in a number of places (Philippians 3:20–21; 1 Thessalonians 4:16–17). The Pauline vision of the profound relationship between individual and cosmic eschatology is also in some important sense missed by Davies, due not least to his emphasis on the *revelation* of believers and not their *resurrection* as such. Put differently, this view is untenable because it fails to understand the Pauline passages regarding the resurrection in the light of other aspects of Pauline eschatology.

The soul and immortality

Modern theology has difficulty with the concept of the soul for two reasons. The first, already hinted at, has to do with the fact that the unitary view of the human being has been widely accepted. The second is the argument, forwarded by a good number of theologians in the twentieth century, that the concept of the immortality of the soul is fundamentally Platonic. Let us take the second objection first, leaving the first to a later stage of the discussion. In the third volume of his systematic theology, Wolfhart Pannenberg addresses the view that the concept of the immortality of the soul is the result of the Platonizing of theology by examining the differences between the Platonic and theological accounts. In contradistinction from Plato's view of the deity of the soul, Christian theology maintains that the soul is a creature. Put differently, the important distinction between eternality and immortality must not be missed. In the Christian tradition, the soul is not eternal but is created immortal. Furthermore, immortality is not a quality intrinsic to the nature of the soul but is a 'gift of grace from God'.[13] The second distinction touches upon the unitary view of man: 'the soul is not on its own the true person as if the body were a burdensome appendage or prison'.[14] The human being, according to the Christian tradition, is a unity of body and soul. And finally, the Christian tradition speaks primarily of resurrection and not of the immortality of the *soul* as such.

The fact that the New Testament says little about the intermediate state has led some theologians to conclude that this concept is the result of Greek influence. Evangelical theologians like Anthony Hoekema, however, have pointed out that several passages in the New Testament speak about the intermediate state: Luke 23:42–43; Philippians 1:21–23; 2 Corinthians 5:6–8. In the first passage, Jesus said to the repentant thief about to be crucified, 'today you will be with me in paradise' (Luke 23:43). 'Paradise' should be understood as a reference to heaven, consistent with the way in which it is used in the rest of the New Testament (1 Corinthians 12:4; Revelation 2:7). Furthermore, the promise of Jesus is said to take place immediately upon the death of the thief, and its fulfilment should not be seen as taking place only at the *parousia*. In the second passage, Paul writes that for him to die is gain and expresses his desire to depart from this world so he can be with Christ. The two infinitives in the statement have a single preceding definite article, thereby denoting that departing and being with Christ are two aspects of the same event. In the third passage (2 Corinthians 5:6–8), Paul's statement, 'to be away from the body and at home with the Lord', refers to the intermediate state. Several other passages that allude to the intermediate state can also be found in the New Testament: for example, the parable of the rich man and Lazarus (Luke 16:22–23), and the statement that persecutors of Christ's disciples cannot 'kill the soul' (Matthew 10:28). All these passages have convinced some evangelical theologians that, difficulties notwithstanding, the idea of the intermediate state is clearly alluded to in the New Testament.

How then can we square our insistence on the unitary view of man with the concept of the intermediate state, which requires us to think of disembodied existence? One way in which we can begin to answer this question is to look at the disintegrating effect of sin. In his Harvard essay on the 'Immortality of the Soul', Orthodox theologian Georges Florovsky writes thus about the damaging effect of sin:

> The very structure of man becomes unstable. The 'union' of soul and
> the body becomes insecure. The soul loses its vital power, is no more
> able to quicken the body. The body is turned into the tomb and prison of
> the soul. And physical death becomes inevitable. The body and the soul
> are no longer, as it were, secured or adjusted to each other.[15]

Sin therefore brings about such a corruption to the human nature that it disrupts the unity of the soul and the body. Another way of approaching this question is to argue that, like chemical compounds, body and soul can be broken down in certain conditions. Evangelical theologians like Millard Erickson have postulated a temporary separation of the body and soul at death. This separation, brought about by sin, must be understood in the light of the original unity. Other evangelical thinkers have used matter and energy to bring out the same point.[16] But the separation of the body from the soul, introduced by death, is temporary, for at the resurrection, the two will be brought together again.

Resurrection
The centrality of the resurrection
The concept of the resurrection of the dead is unique to Christianity and cannot be found in the religions and philosophies

of Asia. Most Asian religions gravitate towards the idea of the reincarnation or rebirth of individuals according to what they have done in their previous lives. The resurrection of the dead is the essence of biblical individual eschatology. As we have seen, belief in the resurrection can be traced to the Old Testament. In Isaiah 26:19, we read:

> But your dead will live;
>   their bodies will rise.
> You who dwell in the dust,
>   wake up and shout for joy.
> Your dew is like the dew of the morning;
>   the earth will give birth to her dead.

The same expectation of the resurrection is found in the book of Daniel (12:2), which speaks of the resurrection of both the wicked and the righteous. The idea of the resurrection can also be found in Ezekiel:

> Therefore prophesy and say to them: 'This is what the Sovereign LORD says: O my people, I am going to open your graves and bring you up from them; I will bring you back to the land of Israel. Then you, my people, will know that I am the LORD, when I open your graves and bring you up from them. I will put my Spirit in you and you will live, and I will settle you in your own land. Then you will know that I the LORD have spoken, and I have done it, declares the LORD.' (Ezekiel 37:12–14)

The continuity between the Old Testament and the teaching of Jesus is instanced by his exchanges with the Sadducees, who denied the resurrection. Jesus defended the idea of the resurrection on the basis of the Old Testament teaching: 'Now about the dead rising – have you not read in the book of Moses, in the account of the bush, how God said to him, "I am the God of Abraham, the God of Isaac, and the God of Jacob"? He is not the God of the dead, but of the living. You are badly mistaken!' (Mark

12:26–27). Perhaps the clearest statement by Jesus regarding the resurrection is found in John's Gospel:

> I tell you the truth, a time is coming and has now come when the dead will hear the voice of the Son of God, and those who hear will live . . . Do not be amazed at this, for a time is coming when all who are in their graves will hear his voice and come out – those who have done good will rise to live, and those who have done evil will rise to be condemned. (John 5:25, 28–29)

Doubtless, it was the apostle Paul who presented the most detailed account of the resurrection, and we shall look at several of his statements in the course of this discussion (see 1 Corinthians 15; 2 Corinthians 5:1–10; 1 Thessalonians 4:13–16). On the basis of the certainty of God's promise and the character of Christ's redemption, Paul insists that there must be a resurrection: the believer must put on immortality, and corruption must put on incorruption. As we have already seen, for Paul, the resurrection of Christ is constitutive of the resurrection of all who are 'in him', for Christ is the 'firstborn of all creation'. From the standpoint of soteriology, the resurrection is important also because the wages of sin is death, and resurrection, insofar as it is death's reversal, signals also death's defeat.

Christ's resurrection and ours

As already indicated, the resurrection of Christ, insofar as it witnesses to the new creation, is profoundly related to the divine promise to restore what sin has destroyed. It is in this sense that Paul understood Christ to be the new Adam (Romans 5), who will bring about the perfection of the creation. But the full implication of the resurrection of Christ can only be grasped when it is considered within the context of apocalyptic hope of Israel. For only in relation to apocalyptic, with its expectation of the resurrection in the end, can Christ's resurrection be seen as its anticipation.[17] It must be emphasized, however, that the resurrection of Christ does not merely verify the apocalyptic expectation of the resurrection.

In 1 Corinthians 15, Paul does not begin with a general idea of the resurrection and then attempt to relate this to the facitity of the resurrection of Christ. Rather the reverse is true: he validates the hope for the resurrection on the basis of the resurrection of Christ. This is clearly articulated by Paul when he insists that 'if Christ has not been raised, our preaching is useless and so is your faith' (1 Corinthians 15:14). The resurrection of Christ, therefore, cannot be seen as an isolated phenomenon or event somehow unrelated to the history of the world and the community of faith. Rather it is the presupposition of the new community of the redeemed and the new world order.

This means that the resurrection of Christ is *constitutive* of our resurrection. This has been the understanding of the church throughout the centuries. For the early disciples, the resurrection of Jesus Christ, which took place within the context of apocalyptic hopes and expectations, was the divine confirmation of his divine authority. In the resurrection of Christ, the disciples saw that the end has already arrived. Thus, because Christ has been raised from the dead, the apocalyptic *idea* of the general resurrection was transformed into the Christian *hope* in the resurrection.[18] This is seen in the fact that the New Testament does not merely describe Jesus as the 'first to rise from the dead' (Acts 26:23), or the 'firstborn from among the dead' (Colossians 1:18). It emphatically declares Jesus as the one whose resurrection life we shall all share, so that we too might receive the 'newness of life' (Romans 6:4–5). To put this differently, the resurrection of Christ is itself an eschatological event, the basis and beginning of the eschatological resurrection of believers. When the disciples proclaim the resurrection, they were 'not preaching a doctrine, a mere hope for the future. They were proclaiming an event in the present which *guaranteed* the future. They were preaching *in Jesus* the resurrection from the dead.'[19]

The nature of the resurrected body
The New Testament teaches that the resurrection will be bodily in nature. One of the clearest statements regarding this is found in

Paul's letter to the Romans, where the apostle writes, 'And if the Spirit of him who raised Jesus from the dead is living in you, he who raised Christ from the dead will also give life to your mortal bodies through his Spirit, who lives in you' (8:11). This belief is also clearly articulated in the creeds of the church, especially the Apostles' Creed. But what does it mean to say that the resurrection of the dead will have a bodily character? What is the nature of the resurrected body? There are many philosophical problems related to the notion of the resurrection, especially pertaining to the question of identity. Biological science has shown that the cells of the human body undergo a complete change every seven years. This means that if biological cells were the basis of the identity of the person, the adult would not be the same person he or she was at birth. What about the resurrected body? Difficulties in conceiving the resurrected body also abound when we ask questions such as the following. What would the resurrected body of a child who died at birth be like? What about someone who died in old age? What about the resurrected bodies of the Christians martyrs who have been torn apart by wild beasts in the Roman Colosseum or those who perished in China's Cultural Revolution?

In an attempt to answer such questions, some have turned to the narratives concerning the resurrected Christ in order to try to glean from them an idea of what the resurrected body will be like. But the picture that emerges is often enigmatic and incoherent. The physicality of the resurrected body of Jesus is seen in the fact that it bore the physical marks of the crucifixion and that it could be handled (John 20:27). There are also references of the resurrected Christ sharing a meal with his disciples (Luke 24:28-31; John 21:9-15). Yet the same Jesus could appear and disappear at will, and has the ability to walk through walls! Although the picture is unclear, what it attests unequivocally is the fact that the resurrected Jesus is the same Jesus whom the disciples knew, the same Jesus who was crucified, died and buried. The main point stressed here is the identity of the resurrected Christ. The accounts of the resurrected Christ also point to the continuities and discontinu-

ities between the pre-resurrection and post-resurrection bodies of
Jesus Christ. The continuities are symbolized by the marks that
the resurrected body of Christ still bears and the fact that it can
impact the physical senses. The discontinuities are to be found in
the fact that Christ's resurrected body has undergone such a
radical transformation that it now possesses powers it did not
possess before. As Ladd puts it, the resurrected body of Christ is
corporeal enough to show his wounds and immaterial enough to
pass through closed doors.[20]

Theologians both past and present have attempted to speculate
about the nature of the resurrected body. The problem with these
approaches, as we shall see, has to do with the fact that they envision the resurrected body in too physical terms. Augustine, for
instance, famously maintained that in order for the resurrection to
be authentic, the same physical bodies that have been laid to rest
in the dust must be raised. This view is quite common among theologians in the early centuries, and its most elaborate explication
can probably be traced to one of the Cappadocian Fathers,
Gregory of Nyssa. Gregory taught that when dead bodies decay,
their elements dissipate into the environment around them, and
over time, they lose their identities as they merge with nature.
How then can the same bodies be reconstituted at the resurrection? Gregory's answer lies in the soul, which he defines as 'an
essence created, and living, and intellectual, transmitting from
itself to an organised sentient body the power of living and of
grasping objects of sense, as long as natural constitution capable
of this holds together'.[21] The soul keeps track of where in the
environment the bodily atoms of a person have migrated after
death, and on the day of the resurrection summons them from a
form of inventory, so that the original body may be reassembled.
The soul will not make the mistake of mixing together parts
of different bodies because 'she always remembers her own as it
was when compact in bodily form, and after dissolution she
never makes any mistake about it, led by marks still clinging to
the remains'.[22]

Paul Helm has rightly argued that such physicalist conceptions of the resurrection are untenable simply because Paul spoke of the resurrected body as a 'spiritual body', and stressed its incorruptibility. This surely must mean that however we may conceive of the resurrected body, it must be more than simply a reconstitution of the physical body. The Corinthians to whom Paul wrote also speculated about the nature of the resurrected body. Anticipating their questions, Paul wrote in 1 Corinthians 15:35, 'But someone may ask, "How are the dead raised? With what kind of body will they come?"' Paul uses a set of antitheses to describe the resurrected body: 'The body that is sown is perishable, it is raised imperishable; it is sown in dishonour, it is raised in glory; it is sown in weakness, it is raised in power; it is sown a natural body, it is raised a spiritual body' (1 Corinthians 15:42–44).

Although Paul is certain that at the resurrection, the same person who has died will be raised, he maintains that there are radical discontinuities between the present physical body and the resurrected body. To further emphasize the difference, Paul uses the enigmatic term 'spiritual body' (sōma pneumatikos) to describe the resurrected body (1 Corinthians 15:44). The term seems to indicate that there will be a bodily reality of some kind in the resurrection, but that it is not just a simple reconstitution of the current physical body. Rather it will be a transformation of the physical body, its metamorphosis or transfiguration. Hans Schwarz is right to say that the 'otherness' of the resurrection 'makes it difficult to talk about'.[23] What is clear from Paul's description is that the resurrection – as new creation – entails fundamental and radical change from the present condition, a change that involves the whole being. This is what the stark Pauline antitheses mentioned above bring out.

Resurrection of the righteous and the wicked

Before we take leave of the discussion on the resurrection, there is one more issue that must be addressed; namely whether the resurrection is *universal*, involving *both* the righteous and the wicked. To

be sure, most references to the resurrection in the New Testament
have to do with the resurrection of believers, and some passages in
the Old Testament, especially Isaiah 26:19, even speak of the resurrection as a reward. Several of Jesus' statements about the
resurrection refer specifically to that of believers. For example, in
John 11:25–26, Jesus said to Martha, 'I am the resurrection and the
life. He who believes in me will live, even though he dies; and
whoever lives and believes in me will never die.' As a matter of
fact, neither in the Synoptic Gospels nor in Paul's writings do we
find references to the resurrection of unbelievers.

There are, however, a number of passages that do speak of the
resurrection of unbelievers, and a fuller account of the biblical
teaching on the resurrection must take them seriously. As we have
seen, in the Old Testament, Daniel speaks explicitly about the resurrection of the wicked (12:2). And in the Gospel of John (5:28–29),
Jesus speaks about the resurrection of both the righteous and the
wicked for judgment in a way reminiscent of the Daniel passage.
The universal nature of the resurrection affirms the biblical idea of
a person as a unitary being, constituting both body and soul.
Because human beings are psychosomatic beings, both salvation
and condemnation involve the *whole* person. In chapter 6, I shall
discuss the two possible destinies that face people, namely, heaven
and hell, and the problems associated with both of them. But first
we shall turn in chapter 5 to two other themes in eschatology –
parousia and judgment.

5

THE COMING OF THE LORD

In this chapter I shall discuss two major topics in traditional Christian eschatology; namely the return of Christ and the final judgment. In some theological circles, these two events are either mythologized or recast and reinterpreted in existentialist terms. Some theologians have idiosyncratically interpreted the *parousia* as a metaphysical idea that signifies the culmination of the evolutionary process of human beings and nature. In similar vein, others have reduced the doctrine of the last judgment to a symbol at best, or, at worst, to the stuff of mythology and folklore. Describing the modern attitude towards the doctrine of the last judgment, Romano Guardini writes, 'The Christian teaching of the Last Judgment is just a myth and must give way to a more serious and advanced view of reality.'[1] Even those theologians who wish to defend the doctrines of the *parousia* and last judgment are ambivalent about the extent to which we can talk about them. Thus, concerning the *parousia*, Helmut Thielicke maintains that to 'speak theologically about the *parousia* is fundamentally to do no more than interpret "rejoicing in the Lord" (Philippians 4:4) . . . No more needs to be said.'[2]

Despite the objections and uncertainties adumbrated above, Scripture's testimony concerning the reality of the return of Christ and last judgment is unequivocal. These important themes are summarized in the historic creeds of the church, thereby bearing witness to the fact that they are not peripheral to the Christian faith. Jesus himself repeatedly spoke about his return in the Synoptic Gospels. In his Olivet Discourse, Jesus told his disciples that at the consummation of the kingdom of God, 'men will see the Son of Man coming in clouds with great power and glory. And he will send his angels and gather his elect from the four winds, from the ends of the earth to the ends of the heavens' (Mark 13:26–27). That, along with the resurrection of the dead, the *parousia* and final judgment, forms an integral part of apostolic preaching and teaching, and is brought out clearly in the writings of Paul. In a forceful statement, Paul brings together resurrection and *parousia*, and delineates their relationship to each other as well as their sequence. 'For as in Adam all die, so in Christ all will be made alive. But each in his own turn: Christ, the firstfruits; then, when he comes, those who belong to him' (1 Corinthians 15:22–23). In his charge to Timothy, Paul relates the ministry to the hope of the *parousia* of Christ: 'I charge you to keep this command without spot or blame until the appearing of our Lord Jesus Christ, which God will bring about in his own time' (1 Timothy 6:13–15). As Ralph Martin has rightly maintained, the 'firm, clear belief in Jesus' visible and glorious return in power, as king and judge, is consistently taught and proclaimed throughout the New Testament'.[3]

The nature of the second coming of Christ
Terms depicting the second advent
The New Testament uses three words – *parousia*, *apokalypsis* and *epiphaneia* – to describe the second advent of Christ, and it is important that we understand what they signify. *Parousia*, which means 'coming', 'arrival' or 'presence', is the word most frequently

used to refer to the return of Christ. The New Testament makes it clear that this event will be a glorious manifestation of Christ, a very public occurrence. At this event, the church will be taken up, the resurrection will take place, and the agents of evil will be destroyed. In 1 Thessalonians 4:15–17, Paul describes the *parousia* in connection with the rapture and resurrection as follows:

> According to the Lord's own word, we tell you that we who are still alive, who are left till the coming of the Lord, will certainly not precede those who have fallen asleep. For the Lord himself will come down from heaven, with a loud command, with the voice of the archangel and with the trumpet call of God, and the dead in Christ will rise first. After that, we who are still alive and are left will be caught up together with them in the clouds to meet the Lord in the air. And so we will be with the Lord for ever.

In his second letter to the Thessalonians, Paul warns about the man of lawlessness, but emphasizes that he will be destroyed at the *parousia*, when Christ returns (2 Thessalonians 2:8).

Taking *parousia* to mean 'presence' has sometimes inadvertently caused some confusion and problems. There are a number of passages in the New Testament where *parousia* can be understood to mean 'presence'. For instance, in Philippians 2:12, Paul contrasts his presence (*parousia*) in the church with his absence (*apousia*) from them.[4] But there are also a number of passages where *parousia* means 'arrival', as is the case in 1 Corinthians 16:17, where Paul rejoices at the arrival (*parousia*) of the envoy from Corinth at Ephesus; and in 2 Corinthians 7:6, where Paul is comforted by the arrival (*parousia*) of Timothy. In regard to Christ, *parousia* must be understood primarily as referring to his arrival rather than his presence. This is clarified in James 5:7–8, where the writer of the epistle exhorts his readers to be patient 'until the *parousia* of the Lord', and to establish their hearts because the '*parousia* of the Lord is at hand'. These verses speak of the coming and arrival of the Lord, not merely his presence. George Ladd explains:

It is not the presence so much as the coming of Christ which is required in the verses we have just discussed. It is at the coming, the advent of Christ, that the dead will be raised and the living caught up; 'presence' does not fit. It is at his coming, his advent, not his presence, that he will be accompanied by his saints. His coming, his advent, will be like a bolt of lightning. The *parousia* of Christ is his second coming, and it will bring both salvation and judgment: salvation to the saints, and judgment of the world.[5]

The second word the New Testament uses to depict the return of Christ is *apokalypsis*, which simply means 'revelation'. In 2 Thessalonians 1:6–7, Paul speaks of the return of Christ in terms of his revelation, during which the righteous will be vindicated and their persecutors punished. 'God is just: He will pay back trouble to those who trouble you and give relief to you who are troubled, and to us as well. This will happen when the Lord Jesus is *revealed* from heaven in blazing fire with his powerful angels.' Peter uses the same term for the return of Christ when he exhorts the Christians in Asia Minor to rejoice, despite the suffering inflicted by their persecutors: 'But rejoice that you participate in the sufferings of Christ, so that you may be overjoyed when his glory is *revealed*' (1 Peter 4:13).

The third word used to refer to the second coming of Christ is *epiphaneia*, which means 'manifestation'. Writing to young Timothy, Paul exhorts him to keep the commandment and be blameless 'until the *appearance* of our Lord Jesus Christ' (1 Timothy 6:13–15). Similarly, towards the end of his life, Paul expresses confidence that he has fought a good fight, and looks forward to receiving his rewards on the day of judgment. He writes to Timothy, 'Now there is in store for me the crown of righteousness, which the Lord, the righteous Judge, will award to me on that day – and not only to me, but also to all who have longed for his *appearing*' (2 Timothy 4:8). And in Titus 2:13–14, Paul articulates the blessed hope of the church when he exhorts Christians to turn away from ungodliness, 'while we wait for the blessed hope – the glorious *appearing* of our great God and Saviour, Jesus Christ'.

The manner of Christ's return

I have already pointed out that the New Testament's testimony regarding the certainty or definiteness of the second coming of Christ is unequivocal and clear. Speaking about the end times in the Olivet Discourse, Jesus refers to his glorious return thus: 'At that time the sign of the Son of Man will appear in the sky, and all the nations of the earth will mourn. They will see the Son of Man coming on the clouds of the sky, with power and great glory' (Matthew 24:30). In that same discourse, Jesus speaks repeatedly about the 'coming of the Son of Man' (verses 27, 37, 39, 42, 44). While Matthew has the most records of Jesus' references to his return, similar statements can also be found in the other Synoptic Gospels. For instance, we find in Mark 13:26 and Luke 21:27 similar declarations that those living in the end times will witness the Son of Man returning in glory. Nor are such statements confined only to the Synoptic Gospels, for John also records Jesus' declarations about his return: 'And if I go and prepare a place for you, I will come back and take you to be with me that you also may be where I am' (14:3). Numerous references to the second advent can be found in the rest of the New Testament, not least in the Pauline corpus. Perhaps the most direct statement by Paul regarding Christ's second coming is 1 Thessalonians 4:15–16. There the apostle states categorically that

> According to the Lord's own word, we tell you that we who are still alive, who are left till the coming of the Lord, will certainly not precede those who have fallen asleep. For the Lord himself will come down from heaven, with a loud command, with the voice of the archangel and with the trumpet call of God, and the dead in Christ will rise first.

Other statements by Paul about the second advent can be found in 1 Corinthians 1:7; 15:23; 1 Thessalonians 2:19; 3:13; 5:23;

2 Thessalonians 1:7–10; 2:1, 8; 1 Timothy 6:14; 2 Timothy 4:1, 8; and Titus 2:13. And in the rest of the New Testament, references to Christ's return are found in Hebrews 9:28; James 5:7–8; 1 Peter 1:7, 13; 2 Peter 1:16; 3:4, 12; 1 John 2:28; and of course in Revelation.

What does the New Testament say about the nature and manner of Christ's return? Ralph Martin succinctly states the traditional view when he writes that 'Christ's coming will be personal, clearly manifest, unmistakable, and visible to all. It will not be hidden or invisibly "spiritual"; this will be the incarnate Son coming, not an invisible working of the Holy Spirit.'[6] This view, however, has been challenged today, not least by those who prefer to think of the kingdom of God within the framework of evolution or a secular idea of progress. According to this view, as expressed by one of its advocates, 'No visible return of Christ to earth is to be expected, but rather the long and steady advance of his spiritual kingdom . . . If our Lord will but complete the spiritual coming that he has begun, there will be no need of a visible advent to make perfect his glory on earth.'[7] This view, however, demands a radical reinterpretation of the passages we have been examining. But as Wayne Grudem has argued so eloquently:

> the passages are far too explicit to allow the idea (once popular in liberal Protestant circles) that Christ himself will not return, but simply that the spirit of Christ, meaning an acceptance of his teaching and an imitation of his lifestyle of love, would increasingly return to earth. It is not his teachings or his style of conduct, but *the Lord himself* who will descend from heaven (1 Thessalonians 4:16).[8]

That the return of Christ will be personal and physical is clearly indicated in the New Testament. In Acts 1:11, the return of Jesus is said to be similar to his departure: '"Men of Galilee," they said, "why do you stand here looking into the sky? This same Jesus, who has been taken from you into heaven, will come back in the same way you have seen him go into heaven."' The 'same Jesus', whom the men had seen ascend in cloud and glory, will return in the same manner on that day.[9] As we have seen above, *parousia* must not be understood primarily to mean 'presence' but 'coming' and 'arrival'. *Parousia* has not to do with Christ's spiritual presence, but with his physical return, as Paul's statement that 'the Lord himself will descend from heaven' (1 Thessalonians 4:16) makes clear. The New Testament also makes it clear that Christ's return will be visible, triumphant and glorious. In Matthew 24:30, Jesus tells his disciples not to be fooled by those who teach that he is to be found in the desert, in the inner chambers or in any special place (24:26), because his return will be unmistakably clear for all to see. Alluding to Matthew 24 and Acts 1, Ralph Martin writes:

> As the angels said at the Ascension, Jesus will return in the same personal, clearly visible, and manifest way in which he ascended to the Father. One will not need to go to special places or to engage in certain activities in order to see him and recognise his coming: it will be clear and unmistakably manifest to all.[10]

The victorious and glorious nature of the second advent is vividly described in the New Testament. Christ will come on the clouds and in glory (Matthew 24:30; Mark 13:26; Luke 21:27), and he will sit on his throne to judge all the nations (Matthew 25:31–46).

What is the difference between the first advent of Christ and the second, between incarnation and *parousia*? Berkouwer rightly cautioned against equating the two events; namely Christ's coming in the flesh and his return in glory. 'It is incorrect', Berkouwer maintains, 'to conclude . . . that both events, past and future, were put on the same level by the early community.'[11] The difference between the two events is broadly summarized in Hebrews 9:28: 'so Christ was sacrificed once to take away the sins of many people; and he will appear a second time, not to bear sin, but to bring salvation to those who are waiting for him'. The contrast between the lowly and humble circumstances of Christ's first coming and the triumphant and glorious nature of his return is

immediately obvious, the former being the first stage of his humiliation and the latter the final stage of his exaltation.

But the passage from Hebrews also describes the different func-
tions associated with Christ's two comings in connection with the
work of the Levitical high priest on the Day of Atonement. The
high priest first appears for the purpose of offering sacrifices for
the atonement of the sins of the people at the altar located in the
courtyard outside the sanctuary. The high priest then enters the
sanctuary with the blood of atonement to intercede for the people
before emerging from the sanctuary and presenting himself once
again to the expectant assembly. Comparing the Levitical system
with the two advents, Philip Hughes writes:

> So also Christ, our unique High Priest of the order of Melchizedek, who
> appeared in the precincts of this world in order 'to put away sin by the
> sacrifice of himself' (v. 26), and then passed from sight into the heavenly
> sanctuary, where he now appears 'in the presence of God on our behalf'
> as our Intercessor and Advocate (v. 24; 7:25; 1 John 2:1), 'will appear a
> second time' to mankind when he comes forth from the true sanctuary
> to proclaim and to perform the completion of salvation for 'those who
> are eagerly waiting for him' (v. 28).[12]

The second coming of Christ is necessary because it completes
the work begun at the incarnation. Through his death on the cross
and his resurrection, Christ has already disarmed the principalities
and powers, defeated them and made an example of them
(Colossians 2:15). But although Christ has already rendered Satan a
decisive defeat, Satan is not yet destroyed. The resurrected Christ
is exalted and enthroned at God's right hand, the kingdom of God
is inaugurated by his ministry, and people continue to be delivered
from bondage and to be transferred from the kingdom of darkness into the kingdom of Christ (Colossians 1:13). But evil is not
eradicated, and the world is still an evil place.

Oscar Cullmann uses the analogy of the Second World War to
envision the 'already' and 'not yet' character of the presence of

God's eschatological kingdom. Two significant events (D-Day and VE-Day) led to victory over Nazi Germany. The tide of the battle turned on D-Day when the allies successfully invaded the continent and began their drive across France. Sporadic fighting still continued, however, and it was not until the enemy had capitulated that the fighting ceased and peace prevailed. Similarly, Jesus has invaded the realm of Satan, and through his death on the cross and resurrection from the dead has rendered Satan a decisive defeat. The tide of the battle has turned. But for now, according to Paul, Christ 'must reign until he has put all his enemies under his feet' (1 Corinthians 15:25). This victory will be achieved only at the *parousia*, when the enemies of God will be crushed forever, and when the Lordship that belongs to Christ will be acknowledged by all.

The time of his coming

The New Testament clearly asserts the fact that Christ is coming again, but it does not reveal when this is going to take place. The Bible in fact discourages speculation regarding the time of Christ's return, and repeatedly insists that none but God alone knows when it will occur. Jesus himself clearly maintains that neither he nor the angels know the time of the *parousia*: 'No-one knows about that day or hour, not even the angels in heaven, nor the Son, but only the Father. Be on guard! Be alert! You do not know when that time will come' (Mark 13:32–33; see also Matthew 24:36–44). Before his ascension, Jesus responded to the curiosity of his disciples concerning the time of the restoration of the kingdom by discouraging speculation: 'It is not for you to know the times or dates the Father has set by his own authority' (Acts 1:7).

Agnosticism concerning the timing of the *parousia* is supplemented by remarks about its unexpected and sudden nature. The period preceding the return will be like 'the days of Noah' (Matthew 24:37), whose ordinariness will lull people to inattention (Matthew 25:1–3; cf. Peter 3:3–4). Sudden destruction will befall a people sedated by their sense of security (1 Thessalonians 5:2–3). As Louis Berkhof has noted, 'The Bible intimates that the measure of surprise at the Second Coming of Christ will be an inverse ratio to the measure of their watchfulness.'[13] 'The human race as a whole', writes Ralph Martin, 'will not be ready for Jesus' return and will be caught by surprise.'[14] 'The day of the Lord', according to the apostle Paul, 'will come like a thief in the night' (1 Thessalonians 5:2).

The last judgment
The certainty of the final judgment

In the Nicene Creed, the church confesses that Jesus Christ will 'come again in glory to judge the living and the dead'. This confession is based on the explicit teaching of the New Testament, where references to the final judgment of the whole human race are replete. In his Olivet Discourse, Jesus says that when he returns, 'All the nations will be gathered before him, and he will separate the people one from another as a shepherd separates the sheep from the goats. He will put the sheep on his right and the goats on his left' (Matthew 25:32–33). Jesus warned that it would be more tolerable for the inhabitants of Sodom and Gomorrah, and of Tyre and Sidon on the day of judgment than for those who heard the gospel but rejected it (Matthew 10:15; 11:22). In 1 Corinthians 4:5, Paul teaches explicitly that when the Lord comes, 'He will bring to light what is hidden in darkness and will expose the motives of men's hearts. At that time, each will receive his praise from God.' Paul emphasizes the universal nature of the final judgment when he says that 'we will *all* stand before God's judgment seat' (Romans 14:10, my emphasis). And again: 'we must *all* appear before the judgment seat of Christ, that each one may receive what is due to him for the things done while in the body, whether good or bad' (2 Corinthians 5:10, my emphasis). Perhaps the most vivid portrayal of the final judgment is John's vision described in Revelation:

> Then I saw a great white throne and him who was seated on it. Earth
> and sky fled from his presence, and there was no place for them. And I
> saw the dead, great and small, standing before the throne, and books
> were opened. Another book was opened, which is the book of life. The
> dead were judged according to what they had done as recorded in the
> books. The sea gave up the dead that were in it, and death and Hades
> gave up the dead that were in them, and each person was judged
> according to what he had done. Then death and Hades were thrown into
> the lake of fire. The lake of fire is the second death. If anyone's name
> was not found written in the book of life, he was thrown into the lake of
> fire. (Revelation 20:11–15)

The final judgment must be seen in relation to and as a culmination of the many precursors in history where God rewards the
righteous and punishes the wicked. God brought deliverance and
blessing to those who were faithful to him, including Noah,
Abraham, Isaac, Jacob, Moses and David. But he also demonstrated
his wrath in judgment against the wicked: the deluge, the disper-
sion of the people who constructed the tower of Babel, and the
judgment of Sodom and Gomorrah. Although the New Testament
clearly points to the eschatological judgment that will take place at
the return of Christ, several passages also make clear that divine
judgment has already begun. In his conversation with Nicodemus,
Jesus asserts that 'Whoever believes in him [God] is not condemned, but whoever does not believe stands condemned already
because he has not believed in the name of God's one and only Son'
(John 3:18). The person of Jesus and his message regarding the
kingdom of God compels the hearer to make a decision that will
determine his destiny. In similar vein, the apostle Paul could
declare that 'there is now no condemnation for those who are in
Christ Jesus, because through Christ Jesus the law of the Spirit of
life set me free from the law of sin and death' (Romans 8:1).

Why is the final judgment necessary? Theologian Helmut
Thielicke argues that the final divine judgment is necessary
because of the inadequate and sometimes perverted nature of

earthly justice.[15] Earthly law judges on the basis of outward appearances, on what it perceives and on what is evident. But it cannot penetrate the heart, which is the seat of intention, and it cannot uncover the true motivations behind certain actions and inaction. Earthly law is administered by finite and sinful human beings, who themselves stand guilty before God. These limitations imply that not everything is clearly perceived as they really are, and instances of self-sacrifice are hidden, while secret crimes remain unpunished. Finally, individuals involved in what Thielicke calls 'supraindividual' guilt are not held legally accountable, since collective guilt and responsibility cannot be subjected to judicial action. Ralph Martin summarizes the discussion as follows: 'Justice is never perfectly done on earth: the good die young; the righteous suffer; the poor are defrauded. But God's word speaks over and over of that great Day of Yahweh, when God's faithful ones will be rewarded and blessed beyond measure, when God's enemies and those who have lived unrighteous lives will be definitively punished.'[16]

The credal declaration that both the living and the dead will be subject to judgment at the *parousia* indicates that this event will take place *after* the general resurrection. It also indicates that the final judgment will be universal, involving every human being in every generation. Just as no-one can escape death, so none can escape the final judgment of God (Acts 10:42; 2 Timothy 4:1; 1 Peter 4:5). This is emphasized by the traditional picture of the 'great assize', with God and Christ sitting on the judgment throne, and with all the nations gathered before them (Matthew 25:31–46). In the final judgment, everything will be made manifest and will come under the verdict of truth. As Roman Catholic theologian Romano Guardini puts it, 'Men and things will appear in their true light, as they are, and every deception will vanish. The inner and most hidden nature, both good and evil, will appear plainly, with all trappings stripped away. Every being will attain to what it is in truth.'[17] Once passed, the judgment will be permanent and irrevocable, and the righteous and the wicked will be sent to their respective final destinations. As Jesus puts it so clearly, the wicked 'will go away to eternal punishment, but the righteous to eternal life' (Matthew 25:46). Louis Berkhof has rightly argued that the final judgment serves as a declaration of the sovereignty and glory of God:

> It will serve the purpose rather of displaying before all rational creatures the declarative glory of God in a formal, forensic act, which magnifies on the one hand his holiness and righteousness, and on the other hand, his grace and mercy. Moreover, it should be borne in mind that the judgment at the last day will differ from that of the death of each individual in more than one respect. It will not be secret, but public; it will not pertain to the soul only, but also to the body; it will not have reference to a single individual, but to all men.[18]

The basis of judgment

The New Testament clearly asserts that judgment will be based primarily on people's relationship with Jesus Christ, the incarnate Son of God. In the Gospel of John, Jesus is recorded as saying, 'There is a judge for the one who rejects me and does not accept my words; that very word which I spoke will condemn him at the last day' (John 12:48). 'Since Jesus is the representative of God, who makes known the revelation in words and deeds given by God,' writes Beasley-Murray, commenting on this verse, 'rejection of his message is rejection of God, and so entails the judgment of God.'[19] Also clear in the Scriptures is that there will be a twofold issue on the day of judgment: acquittal or condemnation. The New Testament uses the idea of justification to refer to the acquittal of the sinner. Space does not allow an in-depth discussion of the meaning of justification. Suffice to say here that justification is the acquittal pronounced by God on the sinner, on the basis of the sinner's objective relationship with Christ. How we respond to Christ will determine our destinies. This is made explicit in John 3:16–21:

> For God so loved the world that he gave his one and only Son, that whoever believes in him shall not perish but have eternal life. For God

did not send his Son into the world to condemn the world, but to save
the world through him. Whoever believes in him is not condemned,
but whoever does not believe stands condemned already because he
has not believed in the name of God's one and only Son. This is the
verdict: Light has come into the world, but men loved darkness instead
of light because their deeds were evil. Everyone who does evil hates
the light, and will not come into the light for fear that his deeds will be
exposed. But whoever lives by the truth comes into the light, so that it
may be seen plainly that what he has done has been done through
God.

In order to understand this passage we must take note of what
it stresses. The passage underscores the fact that God wishes to
redeem the world and not condemn it, and that he has sent his
Son for this purpose. But God's offer of salvation can be appropriated only if the sinner believes in the one whom God has sent.
The fact that God does not intend to condemn anyone can also be
gleaned from the parable of the sheep and the goats (Matthew
25:31–46). To the righteous, the King says, 'Come, you who are
blessed by my Father; take your inheritance, the kingdom prepared for you since the creation of the world.' But the King tells
the wicked, 'Depart from me, you who are cursed, into the eternal
fire prepared for the devil and his angels' (Matthew 25:34, 41). The
first destiny was prepared for human beings, and reflects God's
plan and desire for them, while the second destiny was not
planned for human beings at all.[20]

For Christians who placed their faith in Jesus and lived in obedience to God, the day of judgment will be the day of redemption.
Christians therefore look forward to this day with confidence and
joyful expectation because the coming of the Judge signals their
vindication and salvation. In the face of sporadic persecution,
Peter could urge the Christians in Asia Minor to 'set your hope
fully on the grace to be given you when Jesus Christ is revealed'
(1 Peter 1:13). In the same way, Luke records Jesus as saying to his
disciples, 'When these things begin to take place, stand up and lift

up your heads, because your redemption is drawing near' (Luke 21:28). Paul, looking forward to the glorification, asserts that our present suffering pales in comparison to it.

For Paul, the day of judgment not only signals the liberation of Christians from bondage to sin and death, but the whole creation will also be set free from the corruption and decay brought about by the fall:

> The creation waits in eager expectation for the sons of God to be revealed. For the creation was subjected to frustration, not by its own choice, but by the will of the one who subjected it, in hope that the creation itself will be liberated from its bondage to decay and brought into the glorious freedom of the children of God. (Romans 8:19–21)

The idea that God in the end will transform this fractured creation should not result in a passive attitude towards the ecological crisis of our times. Christians are sometimes accused of this because of their emphasis on the world to come. The transformation of the cosmos, however, must be complemented with the command regarding stewardship. Christians are called to act as God's vice regent, to care for the creation in a way that reflects the care and concern of the Creator.

Christians will be judged by what they have done or failed to do, for they have to give an account of their lives. Underscoring the importance of works of course does not contradict Paul's clear teaching that human beings are justified by faith. This is because for Paul, good deeds are seen as evidence of faith. As Travis explains, 'The only kind of faith which Paul will recognize as real, saving faith is faith which shows its reality by the works it produces – "faith that works through love" (Galatians 5:6).'[21] Among those attitudes and behaviours for which Christians will be judged is the performance of religious activities with impure motives. As Ralph Martin puts it, 'Anything in our life and work that has not really been built solidly on Christ and in harmony with his intentions will be judged.'[22] But although Christians will be judged according to their works, their salvation is secure – they are saved from the wrath and condemnation of God.

Scripture also speaks of a certain category of believers, the so-called lukewarm Christians. It is the clear teaching of Scripture that such believers have a chance of being damned. To the church at Laodicea, Jesus asserts emphatically: 'I know your deeds, that you are neither cold nor hot. I wish you were either one or the other! So, because you are lukewarm – neither hot nor cold – I am about to spit you out of my mouth' (Revelation 3:15–16). Similarly, those who profess faith in Christ, but fail to obey his word will be condemned and excluded from the kingdom:

> Not everyone who says to me, 'Lord, Lord,' will enter the kingdom of
> heaven, but only he who does the will of my Father who is in heaven.
> Many will say to me on that day, 'Lord, Lord, did we not prophesy in
> your name, and in your name drive out demons and perform many
> miracles?' Then I will tell them plainly, 'I never knew you. Away from
> me, you evildoers!' (Matthew 7:21–23)

The Gospel also warns that those who fail to persevere in faith and obedience until the end of their lives will be liable for judgment. 'It will be good for that servant whose master finds him doing so [working] when he returns,' Jesus says. 'I tell you the truth, he will put him in charge of all his possessions.' This is not the case, however, for the servant who beats his fellow-servants and eats and drinks with drunkards. Jesus says the master of the house will return unexpectedly, and will punish that unfaithful servant severely and 'assign him a place with the hypocrites, where there will be weeping and gnashing of teeth' (Matthew 24:46–51).

The judgment of those who have not heard of Christ
What does Scripture teach about the fate of those who have not heard the gospel? Will they be condemned alongside those who

explicitly reject God's offer of salvation? This question has become extremely important in the context of Asia, where the various religions coexist, and are sometimes in conflict with each other. This issue has become significant, however, particularly because of the influence of the pluralist philosophy of religion associated with John Hick – embraced uncritically by some Christian thinkers and theologians in Asia. An eloquent representative of Hickian pluralism is the Indian theologian Stanley Samartha. In *One Christ – Many Religions*, Samartha suggests that '"Brahman is *sat-cit-ananda*" and "God is triune, Father, Son, and Holy Spirit" could be regarded as two responses to the same mystery in two cultural settings.'[23] In an earlier article published in the *Journal of Ecumenical Studies*, Samartha articulates the metaphysical basis for such an assertion: 'Religions are man's responses to the mystery of existence and quests for meaning in the midst of confusion.'[24] Space does not allow for a full discussion of such views. Suffice to say here that the pluralist approach is fundamentally flawed because it is guilty of the very suppositions it berates. In rejecting the dogmatism of exclusivism, it presents itself as uncompromisingly dogmatic. And in rejecting exclusivism it presents a view that is by implication exclusivist: it purports to present the correct view to which everyone must submit.

The Roman Catholic theologian Karl Rahner has attempted to address this question with his concept of the anonymous Christian. According to Rahner, those who have not heard the gospel, but who are open to God through their own religious traditions, are anonymous Christians. They stand a chance of appropriating the salvation made possible by the sacrifice of Christ. Rahner does not present this teaching as dogma, but offers it as a serious speculation regarding the fate of those who have had no chance to hear the gospel. Rahner's approach has been criticized not least for its speculative character and its over-reliance on a particular anthropology.

According to Scripture, God reveals himself through the material creation, making it possible for all human beings to know him, however inferior that knowledge may be. Despite the sound criticism of natural theology forwarded energetically and emphatically by Karl Barth in the first half of the twentieth century, there can be no denying that the New Testament clearly teaches that human beings can know God through his revelation in the created order.[25] In the first chapter of Romans the apostle Paul declares that

> The wrath of God is being revealed from heaven against all the godlessness and wickedness of men who suppress the truth by their wickedness, since what may be known about God is plain to them, because God has made it plain to them. For since the creation of the world God's invisible qualities – his eternal power and divine nature – have been clearly seen, being understood from what has been made, so that men are without excuse . . . Although they know God's righteous decree that those who do such things deserve death, they not only continue to do these very things but also approve of those who practise them. (Romans 1:18–20, 32)

In his exposition of these verses in Romans, the Reformer John Calvin argues that human beings ought to know God through 'the structure of the world and the most splendid ordering of the elements',[26] and they ought to glorify him. Calvin continues by stressing that although God is himself invisible, 'since His majesty shines forth in all His works and in all His creatures, men ought to have acknowledged him in these, for they clearly demonstrate their Creator'. The Reformer takes into account the blindness caused by sin, but argues that 'we are not so blind that we can plead ignorance without being convicted of perversity'.[27] Idolatry, which can be defined as a perversion of the knowledge of God, presupposes that human beings do have a true knowledge of God, however vague that knowledge may be. Because of this, men are without excuse.

Furthermore, Scripture also speaks about human conscience and the ability to distinguish right from wrong. This is asserted in Paul's letter to the Romans:

Indeed, when Gentiles, who do not have the law, do by nature things required by the law, they are a law for themselves, even though they do not have the law, since they show that the requirements of the law are written on their hearts, their consciences also bearing witness, and their thoughts now accusing, now even defending them. (Romans 2:14–15)

Paul then relates this to the final judgment when 'God will judge men's secrets through Jesus Christ, as my gospel declares' (Romans 2:16). Paul seems to be arguing that although all judgments have their basis in Christ, not all have explicit faith in Christ as their criterion. In making such an assertion, Paul is not contradicting himself or devaluing the gospel. Rather he is demonstrating that the gospel operates on wider determinants. James Dunn explains this as follows:

The introduction of the gospel as criterion is not at odds with the preceding argument, as though in speaking of divine judgment Paul suddenly narrows that much broader criterion with which he has been operating to the narrower one of faith in Christ. On the contrary, his point is precisely that his gospel operates with those broader factors, with faith in Christ seen as of a piece with a less well defined responsiveness to the Creator.[28]

Conclusion

The doctrines of the second coming and final judgment are unique to the Christian faith. The closest resemblance to these biblical visions is perhaps found in Islam, which teaches that Jesus will return to defeat the Antichrist (Dajjal), die, be raised from the dead, and be present at the final judgment (see the Koran, Surat Maryam 19:33–34; Surat Zukhruf 43:61). Most Eastern religions, because of their non-linear philosophy of history, do not have an idea of an ultimate judgment at history's end. In Chinese philosophy and religions, there are ideas of judgment and punishment, but the cyclical view of history they espouse has made the idea of reincarnation central to their system of beliefs. The same is the case for Hinduism. I shall allude to them in the next two chapters as we examine individual and cosmic eschatologies.

6

THE PARTING OF WAYS

Almost every religion has a metaphysic of the afterlife in its belief system. In the Chinese belief system(s), there are many different views on what the life hereafter is like. Many Chinese believe in reincarnation, which postulates that a person could be reincarnated as either a dog or a prince, depending on what he does in his present life. The Chinese may have adopted this belief from India via Buddhism. Belief in reincarnation is universal in the religious traditions of India. The idea that the soul/spirit, *atman*, is trapped in the misery of *samsara*, the continuous cycle of existence, is predominant in Hinduism. *Atman* submits to the law of karma and migrates again and again from life to life, birth to birth. In Buddhism, reincarnation is generally also understood as the soul's subjection to the law of karma. A person is reincarnated in good forms of existence through good deeds, and evil forms through evil deeds. To the Buddhist, there are five places for reincarnation: (1) hell, (2) the animal world, (3) the realms of ghosts, (4) the human world and (5) the divine realm. Gods and humans are therefore merely different forms of the reincarnation of creatures that have performed good deeds. Salvation takes place when *nirvana* is achieved. As the complete extinction of the volitional drive that expresses itself in greed and hatred, *nirvana* signals the liberation of the individual from the cycle of births and rebirths.

In Christian individual eschatology the 'afterlife' is understood in terms of the resurrection. Christian eschatology speaks of the final state, by which is meant the particular state in which an individual will be consigned after the final judgment. The general resurrection, which will occur at the close of the age, implies that all humans will be simultaneously subjected to judgment and assigned to their respective destinies. In this chapter, I shall examine the biblical doctrines of heaven and hell – the respective destinies of the righteous and the wicked – and address some of the speculations and misinformation related to these topics.

The final state of the righteous
Issues regarding heaven

Although heaven has a firm place in the Christian tradition as a concept that denotes the future of the righteous, it often eludes the most resplendent of imaginations. What exactly is heaven like? In *The Weight of Glory and Other Addresses*, C. S. Lewis compares our attempts to envision and describe heaven with the efforts of a wretched schoolboy who is forced to labour on the details of grammar and syntax while the joys of poetry elude him. 'The Christian', Lewis writes,

> in relation to Heaven, is in very much the same position as this schoolboy.
> Those who have attained everlasting life in the vision of God doubtless
> know very well that it is no mere bribe, but the very consummation of
> their earthly discipleship; but we who have not yet attained it cannot
> know this . . . [P]oetry replaces grammar, gospel replaces law, longing
> transforms obedience, as gradually as the tide lifts a grounded ship.[1]

Theologically, one of the issues being debated is whether heaven is a state or a place. The fundamental understanding of heaven as intimate communion with God or as the presence of God does not require it to be a place. Since God who is Spirit does not occupy space, and since space belongs to this present world, it would seem that heaven has to do with a condition rather than a specific locale. However, it is clear that the Bible does not speak of the immortality of the soul as such but of the resurrection of the body. This must mean that we cannot avoid the concept of place when we think of heaven. This topic will be taken up when I discuss the new creation in the next chapter.

The second issue has to do with life in heaven. How many of our experiences in this life will continue in heaven? Jesus in the Gospels alludes to the fact that in the life hereafter, there will be no marrying or giving in marriage (Matthew 22:30; Mark 12:25; Luke 20:35), thereby implying that there will be no sex in heaven. Ulrich Simon thinks that this is because 'the propagation of the species is no longer required' in heaven.[2] Another issue has to do with whether there will be progress, growth and development in heaven. Put differently, are there sound reasons to embrace the static view of heaven proposed by those theologians who are influenced by Greek philosophy? But if there is growth in heaven, is there also the corresponding frustration that often accompanies such growth in this life?[3] Finally, will there be varying rewards in heaven? If this is the case, 'would not the joy of heaven be reduced by one's awareness of the differences and the constant reminder that one might have been more faithful?'[4] And will there not be envy and rivalry among the righteous in heaven?

The nature of heaven

The New Testament describes the destiny of the righteous in metaphorical language and does not attempt to answer all our questions concerning heaven. The New Testament therefore does not provide an encyclopaedic description of heaven to satisfy our curiosity, but assures us that the life to come is certain for believers. Any attempt to speculate about heaven in order to fill the gaps in our knowledge will prove to be futile, because heaven is a reality beyond the grasp of our imagination. However the Bible does provide some data from which we may construct a sufficiently clear, albeit incomplete, picture of heaven. Scripture uses the term 'heaven' in several different senses. The expression 'heaven and earth' refers to the entire universe, and 'heaven' is here used in the cosmological sense. In the creation story, for instance, we are told that 'In the beginning God created the heavens and the earth' (Genesis 1:1). 'Heaven' is also sometimes used to refer to God himself. For example, upon returning to his father, the prodigal son declares, 'I have sinned against heaven and against you' (Luke 15:18, 21). The Gospel of Matthew, because it was written primarily for a Jewish audience, often uses 'heaven' as a synonym of Yahweh.

It is the third meaning of 'heaven' that is of great importance in this discussion. When Jesus taught his disciples to pray, 'Our Father, who art in heaven', 'heaven' refers to the dwelling place of God. This expression is repeated often in the Gospels.[5] Jesus is said to come from heaven: 'No-one has ever gone into heaven except the one who came from heaven – the Son of Man' (John 3:13). At the ascension, Jesus returns to heaven to prepare a place for his disciples, and he will return to take them there (John 14:1–4). Concerning the return of Christ, Paul writes, 'For the Lord himself will come down from heaven, with a loud command, with the voice of the archangel and with the trumpet call of God, and the dead in Christ will rise first' (1 Thessalonians 4:16). Heaven is the place where believers will reside forever, since it is God's abode. Revelation 21:3 depicts heaven as analogous to the tabernacle of the Old Testament, a tent in which God dwelt among the people of Israel. Heaven is thus depicted as the presence of God: 'And I heard a loud voice from the throne saying, "Now the dwelling of God is with men, and he will live with them."'

As Revelation 21:4 makes clear, heaven will be a place where all suffering and evil will be removed: 'He will wipe every tear from their eyes. There will be no more death or mourning or crying or pain, for the old order of things has passed away.' It will be a place where the glory of God will be made fully manifest. This theme is often associated with the second coming of Christ and the consummation of the kingdom of God. In Mark, Jesus tells the multitude that he will come 'in his Father's glory with the holy angels' (8:38). The glory of the Lord will shine throughout heaven, making it a place of unimaginable brilliance and splendour. Perhaps the most vivid image of this is found in the description of the new Jerusalem in Revelation 21:18–21:

> The wall was made of jasper, and the city of pure gold, as pure as glass. The foundations of the city walls were decorated with every kind of precious stone. The first foundation was jasper, the second sapphire, the third chalcedony, the fourth emerald, the fifth sardonyx, the sixth carnelian, the seventh chrysolite, the eighth beryl, the ninth topaz, the tenth chrysoprase, the eleventh jacinth, and the twelfth amethyst. The twelve gates were twelve pearls, each gate made of a single pearl. The great street of the city was of pure gold, like transparent glass.

The description is of course symbolic. On the significance of the description of 'transparent glass', for instance, John Walvoord writes that 'the constant mention of transparency indicates that the city is designed to transmit the glory of God in the form of light without hindrance'.[6]

From what has been said so far it should be clear that heaven has a fundamentally redemptive character. It is not a natural process or the outcome of human effort. As Paul Helm has put it, 'Heaven is made possible only by the work of Christ and by personal union with him through faith.'[7] Christ humbled himself and died a sacrificial death on the cross for the sin of the world, thereby making the salvation of God available to all men. Thus Christ has brought life and immortality to light through the gospel (2 Timothy 1:10), and has gone to prepare a place for God's people (John 14:2). Because of Christ's victory over sin and death, those who put their faith in him, though mortal, will put on immortality (1 Corinthians 15:33). Death has been conquered by Christ in the resurrection and swallowed up in victory (1 Corinthians 15:54).

Although heaven is a future reality, believers in Christ already have a foretaste of it now. Writing to the Ephesians, Paul could therefore say that the church in Ephesus was already seated in the heavenly places in Christ (Ephesians 2:6). Commenting on this passage, John Calvin writes:

> What he [Paul] declares of the resurrection and the session in heaven, is not yet seen with the eyes. Yet, as if those blessings were already in our possession, he states that they have been conferred on us, so that he may declare the change in our condition, when we were led from Adam to Christ. It is as if he said that we had been transferred from the deepest hell to heaven itself. And certainly, although, as respects ourselves, our salvation is still hidden in hope, yet in Christ we possess blessed immortality and glory.[8]

Life in heaven

What will life in heaven be like? Although the biblical data on this topic are slight, they do allow us some glimpses of the nature of our future existence. One aspect of life in heaven is rest. The concept of rest is employed by the writer of Hebrews to refer to the eschatological salvation that believers will enjoy if they persevere in their earthly pilgrimage (Hebrews 3:7–11). This passage refers to three 'rests': (1) the rest of the Sabbath, during which God rested from all his works; (2) the rest of the Promised Land, where the Israelites rested from their toil and misery; and (3) the true rest of the kingdom of heaven, where believers will rest from all their labour and hardship.[9] The writer of Hebrews exhorts believers to strive to enter the true rest of heaven: 'There remains, then, a Sabbath-rest for the people of God; for anyone who enters God's rest also rests from his own work, just as God did from his. Let us, therefore, make every effort to enter that rest, so that no-one will fall by following their example of disobedience' (4:9–11).

Does the eschatological rest of heaven mean the cessation of all work? A number of passages seem to require this conclusion. Revelation 14:13 asserts that those who die in the Lord will be

allowed to rest from their labour on account of the good deeds
they have performed on earth. Such passages have prompted the
conclusion that 'those who live in Heaven do not act; they see and
they hear; they are at peace and they rest'.[10] Other passages,
however, suggest differently. In the Gospel of John, Jesus is
recorded as saying, 'My Father is always at his work to this very
day, and I, too, am working' (5:17). Ulrich Simon maintains that
'this doctrine of the ever-working God affects the whole'.[11] The
work to which Jesus refers in this Johannine passage, however, is
the work of redemption and judgment.[12] Believers on earth are to
be fellow-workers of God (1 Corinthians 3:9), sharing in this
'strange work' of God (Isaiah 28:21); but how this relates to the
work of the righteous in heaven is unclear. Be that as it may, it is
reasonable to speculate that the work the righteous perform in
heaven is service to God. 'So heaven is not rest from work', argued
Helm, 'but from opposition from the exhausting effort that comes
from fighting against these powers and forces which would, if they
could, stifle the life of God in the soul.'[13]

Perhaps work in heaven can best be described as liturgical.
Worship is an important facet of life in heaven, as the vivid description of the great multitude in heaven and the twenty-four elders in
Revelation 19 makes clear (19:1–4). Sketches of heaven can be
gleaned from Isaiah, especially chapter 6, which recounts a vision
of God sitting on the throne and the doxology of the seraph:

> Holy, holy, holy is the LORD Almighty;
>   the whole earth is full of his glory.
>   (6:3)

Ulrich Simon describes heaven as a Sabbath in which the
redeemed of the Lord, after suffering many trials and persecutions, will rejoice continually in the presence of the Lord:

> The Sabbath in heaven is a continual feast day and the participants are
> released from the burden of toil to be free for the worship of God. This is

the real meaning behind the idea of the eternal Sabbath and its peace. The four beasts in the Apocalypse (4:8), like the Seraphim in Isaiah 6, offer endless homage to the true God: they make Sabbath, without day and night. The twenty-four elders lead the heavenly church in the ministry of Glory (6:4, 10; 5:11ff.), for it is in the performance of worship that the whole creation is united and continues its active life in perfection.[14]

The final state of the wicked
Issues concerning hell
The doctrine of the eternal punishment of the wicked has come under severe criticism by modern theologians. Some have opined that the doctrine is an outmoded sub-Christian view of reality and must be rejected.[15] Together with angels and demons, this doctrine must be demythologized. From the theological angle, this doctrine is often rejected because it is seen as an insoluble and blatant contradiction of the biblical portrayal of love as the cardinal characteristic of the nature of God. The traditional view of the conscious eternal punishment of the wicked portrays rather a tyrannical and sadistic deity who metes out eternal punishment for temporal sins. These objections have resulted in a number of alternatives to the traditional view of hell. A view gaining acceptance in some circles is universalism, which postulates that in the end, God's salvation will reach every human being, and all will be saved. It is pertinent to note that universalism is established on the understanding that God is love. The loving God, it is argued, cannot possibly send any of his rational creatures to hell.

Another approach to the doctrine of hell is the metaphorical view, which argues that the graphic descriptions of hell found in the New Testament should not be taken literally. The New Testament uses hyperbole or colourful language to present a vivid picture of hell and to bring home the truth regarding the destiny of the wicked. It is therefore important that we do not confuse 'the vehicle that brings the truth with the message'.[16] As we shall see, this view is in fact not inimical to the traditional view. It carefully qualifies the language about hell in both Scripture and theology to prevent an over-literal interpretation. Another approach gaining assent among evangelicals is annihilationism, or 'conditional immortality'. Canadian theologian, Clark Pinnock, has ably argued this view and in the next subsection we shall examine his proposals in greater detail. Pinnock maintains that 'the traditional view of hell has been a stumbling block for believers and an effective weapon in the hands of sceptics for use against the faith'.[17] Pinnock proposes that the fate of the wicked is not eternal conscious punishment but destruction or annihilation, and discusses several scriptural passages to prove his position.

What is pertinent is that most of these theologians argue their positions on the basis of their interpretation of key passages in the Bible. In 2000, InterVarsity Press published a dialogue between two evangelical theologians, Edward William Fudge and Robert A. Peterson, on this topic.[18] Fudge holds the conditional view of hell, and his book *The Fire That Consumes: The Biblical Case for Conditional Immortality* (1994) is an able and detailed defence of his position.[19] Peterson argues in favour of the traditional view, and summarizes the position he carefully delineates in *Hell on Trial: The Case for Eternal Punishment* (1995).[20] In the dialogue, both theologians commandeered numerous passages from both the Old and the New Testaments to support their respective positions. In the final analysis, however, the position presented must answer not only to the criterion of Scripture (this is imperative); it must also be able to satisfy systematic concerns, or, to put it differently, it must answer to the criterion of coherence. That is to say, a theology of hell – whether traditional or revisionist – should correspond not just to what specific passages have to say about the topic, but also to what the Bible has to say about God, man and eschatology.

Conditional immortality

Before I discuss the traditional view, let us examine briefly its most popular alternative, annihilationism, or conditional immortality. I shall trace the arguments of one of its most eloquent proponents,

Clark Pinnock. 'Of all the articles of theology that have troubled the human conscience over the centuries', writes Pinnock in his clear and cogent defence of conditional immortality, 'I suppose few have caused any greater anxiety than the received interpretation of hell as everlasting conscious punishment in body and soul.'[21] The traditional view of hell, Pinnock argues, cannot be reconciled with the revelation of God in Jesus Christ, who is a God of boundless mercy. The traditional view, according to him, presents a cruel and vindictive deity who tortures people eternally. Together with the Roman Catholic theologian Hans Küng, Pinnock asks, 'What would we think of a human being who satisfied his thirst for revenge so implacably and insatiably?'[22] Furthermore, the traditional doctrine contradicts the moral goodness of God. Pinnock maintains that this picture of torturing people eternally is more easily associated with Satan than with the biblical God. What human crime, he asks, could deserve everlasting torment? Pinnock concludes that the 'traditional view of hell is a very disturbing concept that needs reconsideration'.[23]

The Bible does present a picture of hell as a final and irreversible destruction, and as the definitive end of the wicked person's relationship with God. But when the Bible speaks about the final fate of the wicked, it uses the language of death and destruction, of ruin and perishing. The imagery of fire, when placed alongside that of destruction, suggests annihilation. The reason why such annihilation is described as '*eternal* punishment' is that it is final and irreversible. 'Eternal punishment' therefore does not mean the eternal, *conscious* punishment of the impenitent wicked, which is taught by the traditional view. On the basis of this interpretation, Pinnock could confidently assert that 'although there are many good reasons for questioning the traditional view of the nature of hell, the most important reason is the fact that the Bible does not teach it. Contrary to the loud claims of the traditionalists, it is not a biblical doctrine.'[24]

Pinnock, by his exegesis of some key passages from both the Old and New Testaments, tries to show that the Bible teaches conditional immortality. He refers to Psalm 37 and points out that in verse 2, the psalmist describes the fate of the wicked as analogous to the fading of the grass or the withering of the herb. The psalmist goes on to say that the wicked will be cut off and perish (verses 9–10), that they will vanish like smoke (verse 20) and be destroyed (verse 38). Pinnock cites Malachi 4, which says that the wicked will 'be stubble', that they will 'burn like a furnace'. 'Not a root or a branch will be left to them' (Malachi 4:1). These statements suggest that the wicked will in the end be destroyed or annihilated. Pinnock maintains that the imagery of destruction and perishing in the Old Testament 'sets the tone for the New Testament doctrine'.

According to Pinnock, Jesus deliberately refrained from creating a picture of hell and was contented to allude to the Old Testament depiction of hell as final destruction. Annihilation was clearly meant, Pinnock maintains, when Jesus warned about God's ability to destroy both body and soul in hell (Matthew 10:28) when he spoke about the fate that awaited the wicked. Jesus was following the terms John the Baptist used when he described the wicked as a tree that 'will be cut down and thrown into the fire' (Matthew 3:10). The wicked will be burned up like weeds thrown into the fire (Matthew 13:30, 42, 49–50), and they will be like rubbish thrown into Gehenna, the valley outside Jerusalem where sacrifices were offered to Moloch. Pinnock ends his survey with this conclusion: 'the impression Jesus leaves us with is a strong one: The impenitent wicked can expect to be destroyed by the wrath of God.'[25] Annihilationism finds much support in the writings of Paul, who speaks of the destiny of the wicked as everlasting destruction. Paul warns that the wicked 'who sows to please his sinful nature, from that nature will reap destruction' (Galatians 6:8). God will destroy the wicked (1 Corinthians 3:17; Philippians 1:28) and the destruction that awaits the unrepentant sinner will be final and everlasting (2 Thessalonians 1:9).

Turning to the rest of the New Testament, Pinnock was able to arrive at the same conclusion. Peter spoke of the 'destruction of ungodly men' on the day of judgment (2 Peter 3:7), and compares this with the destruction of Sodom and Gomorrah, which were burned to ashes (2:6), and with the destruction of the ancient world in the deluge (3:6–7). Similarly Peter asserts that the false teachers who teach 'destructive heresies' and who deny the Lord will bring 'swift destruction upon themselves' (2:1). Hebrews teaches that the wicked who abandoned the faith will likewise be destroyed (10:39). And in the same way, Revelation speaks about the second death that awaits those 'whose names are not found in the Book of Life'; that is, unrepentant sinners (Revelation 20:14–15). Pinnock maintains that '[a] fair person would have to conclude from such texts that the Bible can reasonably be read to teach the final destruction of the wicked. It is shocking to be told that there is no basis for thinking this way.'[26] Without dogmatizing this position, John Stott opines that 'the ultimate annihilation of the wicked should at least be accepted as a legitimate, biblically founded alternative to their eternal conscious torment'.[27]

Apart from presenting the biblical evidence for conditional immortality, Pinnock also offers some systematic reasons for holding this position, and I shall discuss them very briefly here. First Pinnock rightly points out that the Bible, unlike Greek philosophy, does not teach natural immortality. The capacity to live forever is not the inherent possession of human nature (or the human soul), but is a gift from God. According to Pinnock, the Bible teaches conditionalism – God gives immortality to man, and he can take it away.[28] Secondly Pinnock insists that the traditional view of hell is morally abhorrent and is offensive to our moral sense. The God depicted in the traditional view of hell is a cruel and sadistic torturer and is an antithesis to the biblical God of love. For Pinnock, then, the traditional view of hell simply fails the moral test.[29] Thirdly the traditional view of hell poses great difficulties regarding the principle of justice, because it portrays an unjust God. 'Let readers ask themselves what lifestyle, what set of actions, would deserve the ultimate of penalties – everlasting conscious punishment?' The eternal conscious punishment of the wicked taught in the traditional view is, according to Pinnock, 'too heavy a sentence and cannot be successfully defended as a just action on God's part. Sending the wicked to everlasting torment would be to treat persons worse, than they could deserve.'[30] Finally Pinnock thinks that the traditional view would result in a cosmological dualism where heaven *and* hell coexist. This fails to take seriously the New Testament statement that God is going to be 'all in all' (1 Corinthians 15:28).

The traditional view

Conditional immortality, it must be emphasized, does take sin and the final judgment seriously. It differs from the traditional view in the way the punishment of the wicked is understood, and rejects the concept of conscious eternal punishment. Some conditionalists maintain that the wicked will be punished for an unspecified period before they are annihilated, while others insist that annihilation will take place immediately after the final judgment. All reject the literal reading of the biblical account of hell frequently associated with the traditional position. In response to conditional immortality, however, the traditional position does not necessarily warrant a naïve literal interpretation of the biblical passages on hell. The traditional view of hell can be constructed and defended without having to adopt or endorse the exegesis and hermeneutics of scholars like John Walvoord.[31] Such approaches are of a piece with popular pictures of hell perpetuated by works like the *Divine Comedy* by Dante Alighieri, which no Christian should affirm today.

The New Testament often uses words symbolically to describe certain realities, and its description of hell is no exception. These descriptions intend to show that God has ordained a terrible end for the wicked, but they are not meant to serve as literal depictions of what that end is like. Thus we find in the New Testament the use of several different images to depict hell. Hell is sometimes described as Gehenna, the wasteland of the Hinnom Valley (Matthew 25:41), and at other times, as a fiery furnace or lake

(Matthew 13:49–50; Revelation 20:15). On other occasions, hell is described as the outer darkness, as is the case in Matthew 8:12, where Jesus warned that while Gentiles will be included in the kingdom, some Jews will be 'thrown outside, into the darkness, where there will be weeping and gnashing of teeth'. These descriptions would be incoherent if they were understood in the literal sense, for, as Crockett rightly points out, 'How could hell be literal fire when it is also described as darkness (Matthew 8:12; 22:13; 25:30; 1 Peter 2:17; Jude 14)?'[32]

The traditional view corresponds more completely to the entire body of the biblical passages concerning hell. Scripture not only speaks of eternal death but of eternal torment as well. In Isaiah 66:24, we read, 'And they will go out and look upon the dead bodies of those who rebelled against me; their worm will not die, nor will their fire be quenched, and they will be loathsome to all mankind.' The same imagery and message is found in the New Testament, especially in the statements made by Jesus about hell (see Mark 9:43–48).

What about those who hold the view that the punishment of the wicked will be temporal? Matthew's Gospel presents a parallel between 'eternal life' and 'eternal punishment' when it states that the wicked will 'go away to eternal punishment, but the righteous to eternal life' (25:46). To understand *aiōnios* differently when predicated to 'punishment' and 'life' respectively is to use the word in an inconsistent and idiosyncratic manner. As F. D. Maurice puts it, 'I did not see how *aiōnios* could mean one thing when it was joined with *kolasis* and another when it was joined with *zōē*.'[33] Commenting on the meaning of 'eternal' in Matthew 25, Augustine wrote:

> If both are 'eternal', it follows necessarily that either both are to be taken as long-lasting but finite, or both as endless and perpetual. The phrases 'eternal punishment' and 'eternal life' are parallel and it would be absurd to use them in one and the same sentence to mean: 'Eternal life will be infinite, while eternal punishment will have an end.' Hence, because the

eternal life of the saints will be endless, the eternal punishment also, for those condemned to it, will assuredly have no end.[34]

The main problem raised by conditionalists regarding the traditional view is the injustice of eternal conscious punishment. How can God punish the sinner for all eternity because of the sins committed in time? To recall Pinnock's objection, such a view would present God as a vindictive and sadistic deity. This objection is not new and is answered – satisfactorily in my view – by theologians like Augustine and Aquinas. Part of the reason why such an objection has become important again today is that it is revitalized by the culture of individualism. Augustine's response therefore is surprisingly relevant. Refusing to reduce sin and sinfulness to isolated and specific acts, Augustine points rather to the complicity of human beings in the original and universal sin of Adam, thereby emphasizing the communality and depth of the sinful condition. The righteousness of eternal punishment poses no problem once the magnitude of original sin and its implications on humanity are fully grasped.[35] Approaching the question from a different angle, Aquinas argues for the justification of eternal punishment on the principle that the higher the person against whom an offence is committed, the graver the offence. It is 'more criminal to strike a head of state than a private citizen'. Since God is of infinite greatness, sin against God is infinite.[36]

Both Pinnock and Stott allege that the traditional view of hell requires a metaphysical dualism antithetical to the biblical vision that ultimately God will be 'all in all' (1 Corinthians 15:28). Pinnock expresses his objections thus:

> The doctrine creates a lurking sense of metaphysical disquiet. History ends so badly under the old scenario. In what is supposed to be the victory of Christ, evil and rebellion continue in hell under conditions of burning and torturing. In what is supposed to be a resolution, heaven and hell go on existing alongside each other forever in everlasting cosmological dualism.[37]

Stott expresses the same unease when he says that the eternal existence of the impenitent in hell 'would be hard to reconcile with the promises of God's final victory' in the New Testament. He concludes that 'it would be easier to hold together the awful reality of hell and the universal reign of God if hell means destruction and the impenitent are no more'.[38]

This is *one* way of understanding what the New Testament means when it says that ultimately God will be 'all in all'. But such an interpretation will encounter difficulties when passages that speak of eternal torment are taken into account. The annihilationist's tack is to gloss over these passages and take them to refer to destruction. Also the annihilationist's difficulty with the traditional view has to do with his or her understanding of hell as the last bastion of rebellion, or, to use Paul Helm's description, 'a demonic colony which has gained unilateral independence from God'.[39] But, as Helm has rightly pointed out, this view of hell does not seem to correspond to the sense of the scriptural passages. If this view is correct, the annihilationist's objections are valid. Hell is a 'breeding ground for further injustice and resentment, for further sin', and God cannot be said to be 'all in all'. But, as Helm has rightly argued, there is no reason to think that hell is 'the sinner's heaven', a 'fool's paradise':

> We are informed that before Christ the Judge every knee shall bow and every tongue confess that Jesus Christ is Lord to the glory of God the Father (Philippians 2:11). And this language implies that the impenitent will recognise the essential justice of their plight. For they too recognise Christ's Lordship, and confess him, not with love and adoration as a Saviour, but as their Lord . . . Because there is full recognition of God's justice, God's character is vindicated, and hence glorified, even by those who in this life have defied him and who suffer for it.[40]

7

A NEW WORLD COMING

Signs of the end

The Bible indicates that the final consummation of the kingdom of God at the second coming of Christ will be preceded by certain events that will serve as signs of the end of history. These signs have become the source of so much speculation about the time of the *parousia* that it is important at the very outset to discuss their nature and significance. The best place to begin is to examine the teachings of Jesus in the Olivet Discourse (Matthew 24; Mark 13). In these passages, Jesus identifies four general features of the period before his return and the consummation of the kingdom: (1) The decline of faith (Matthew 24:11–12; Mark 13:5–6, 21–22); (2) the persecution and global evangelism of the church (Mark 13:9–11, 19); (3) wars and rumours of wars between the nations (Mark 13:7–8; Luke 21:20ff.); and (4) natural catastrophes and upheavals in nature (Mark 13:8, 24–25; cf. Luke 21:11). Although there are similarities between apocalyptic and the Olivet Discourse, the dissimilarities between them are significant. The fundamental motif of the two is different in that while apocalyptic describes unnatural signs, the Olivet Discourse depicts evil in terms of ordinary historical

experiences.[1] The apocalyptists predict that evil will intensify and
chaos will reign in both human social relationships and the natural
order. While in general agreement with this, Jesus expanded this
view to include the kingdom of God, which has already dawned in
this dark and evil age and that will in the end overcome it as the
gospel is proclaimed.

The Olivet Discourse is more complex than it appears to the
cursory reader. Overwhelmed by Jesus' prediction of the destruction of the great temple of Herod, the disciples ask their Master,
'Tell us, when will this happen, and what will be the sign of your
coming and of the end of the age?' (Matthew 24:3). There are two
questions here: the first is concerned with the time of the destruction of the temple, and the second has to do with the time of
Christ's return. Jesus answered both questions, but in such a way
that the first event is tied to the second, thus relating history to
eschatology. The 'desolating sacrilege standing at the holy place'
refers to the introduction of a pagan altar to the holy place of the
temple in Jerusalem by a pagan conqueror in 168 BC, which,
according to Jesus, will be repeated again. This prediction was
fulfilled in AD 70 when the Romans recaptured Jerusalem, dese-
crated the temple and burnt it to the ground. Jesus 'links the
coming judgment of God upon impenitent Israel in AD 70 with the
final catastrophe at the end of the age which will precede his
return (Matthew 24:23–31; Mark 13:21–27)'.[2]

Jesus, however, discourages the 'signs of the times' mentality.
For instance, in Luke 17:20, Jesus emphasizes that 'The kingdom of
God does not come with your careful observation', and he often
refuses to authenticate his ministry with signs. Furthermore, Jesus
repeatedly exhorts his disciples to be watchful, because his return
and the kingdom's consummation will take place suddenly and
without warning. In Mark 13:36–37, we read, 'If he comes suddenly, do not let him find you sleeping. What I say to you, I say to
everyone: "Watch!"' This same warning is made in the parable of
the ten virgins and the parable of the talents (Matthew 25). It
would be a mistake therefore to think that one could tell when the

end would take place by studying the signs in the Olivet Discourse. George Ladd is surely right when he writes:

> *The Olivet Discourse describes no signs by which the end can be calculated.* In fact, they are not eschatological signs at all. The Discourse itself makes this clear. False messiahs will arise; wars will occur; 'but the end is not yet' (Mark 13:7). These events are no signs of an imminent end; they will occur, but the end delays. Rather than being signs of the end, they are only 'the beginning of woes' (Mark 13:8) which will mark the entire age.[3]

Paul warns that in the last days there will be a heightening of evil and godlessness and provides a lengthy catalogue of human wickedness in 2 Timothy 3.

> People will be lovers of themselves, lovers of money, boastful, proud, abusive, disobedient to their parents, ungrateful, unholy, without love, unforgiving, slanderous, without self-control, brutal, not lovers of the good, treacherous, rash, conceited, lovers of pleasure rather than lovers of God – having a form of godliness but denying its power. (2 Timothy 3:2–5)

Paul maintains that the presence of false teachers is indicative of the fact that this movement of decadence and chaos has already begun (3:6–7). This, however, should not lead to the conclusion that the Day of the Lord has already taken place. In his letters to the Thessalonians Paul was at pains to explain that the return of Christ must be distinguished from the precursory signs. Paul argues further that two other signs must appear before the end will occur; namely the great revolt and the appearance of the 'man of lawlessness' (2 Thessalonians 2). Thus although the *parousia* must be distinguished from the signs that must take place in history, it nevertheless stands in relation to those signs and cannot just happen at any moment.

Although Paul did not directly use the term, it is evident that the 'man of lawlessness' about whom he speaks in 2 Thessalonians 2 is the Antichrist.[4] The Antichrist will conduct a massive rebellion against God, his two primary targets being religion and ethics, the essence of human culture. In referring to him as a 'man of lawlessness' (2:3) and the 'lawless one' (2:8), Paul indicates that the Antichrist is the great antinomian, who defies both civil law and the moral law of God. His defiance indeed can be characterized as relativism and anarchy. The Antichrist will lead an anti-God movement with the goal of usurping the place of God himself: 'He will oppose and will exalt himself over everything that is called God or is worshipped, so that he sets himself up in God's temple, proclaiming himself to be God' (2:4). The goal of the Antichrist is unequivocal: he wishes to transfer the worship that belongs to God to himself. As Calvin puts it, 'the Antichrist would seize the things which belong to God alone, his purpose being to exalt himself above every divine power, so that all religion and all worship of God should lie beneath his feet'.[5]

The concept of the Antichrist is also found in Matthew 24, the epistles of John and the book of Revelation. Alluding to the desecration of the temple by Antiochus Epiphanes, described in Daniel 11:31, Jesus predicted a similar event that took place in AD 70 when the Roman armies recaptured Jerusalem. But Jesus pointed beyond this event to the 'eschatological Antichrist who will rise at the end time, of whom both Antiochus and Rome were foreshadowings'.[6] The appearance of the Antichrist will bring about the great tribulation: 'For then there will be great distress, unequalled from the beginning of the world until now – and never to be equalled again' (Matthew 24:21). In Revelation 13, John describes the Antichrist in similar vein. Is John referring to Nero, under whose persecution the church suffered greatly? Like Matthew 24, Revelation 13's depiction of the Antichrist has a double fulfilment. Just as in the Olivet Discourse Jesus had in view both the fall of Jerusalem and the eschatological Antichrist, so in Revelation 13 John sees first Rome and then beyond it the eschatological Antichrist.

There have been numerous attempts to speculate on the identity of the Antichrist in the history of the church. These attempts have not only failed to shed light on the identity of the Antichrist;

they have also created much confusion. It is important we understand that the Antichrist, as anti-God forces in their diverse
manifestations, is a spirit already abroad in our world. This
approach has the advantage of putting in check futile speculations.
As Bruce Milne has commented,

> every denial of God manifests the spirit of antichrist, whether it be formal
> denials of the false teachers or the implicit denials of the great dictators
> and all who aspire to divine authority and despise or destroy human life . . .
> If an antichrist arises in our time or in the next generation whose denial of
> God and Christ assumes something of the impressive form which Paul
> alludes to in 2 Thessalonians, then we may feel some justification for lifting
> up our heads because our redemption has drawn near (Luke 21:28). In the
> meantime we are not to be idle but rather by life and witness confront the
> powers of antichrist abroad in the world in our generation.[7]

The Millennium

The idea of the thousand-year reign of Christ is prevalent in
certain periods of the history of theology and stems from
Christianity's relationship with the Hebraic conception of human
history. Unlike the Ancient Near-Eastern cultures and the Chinese
world-view, the Hebrews early developed a historical consciousness that led them to envision the directionality of history and its
telos (climax). This linear view, as opposed to the circular view
common among Asian cultures, enabled the Hebrews to envision
the end of history that Yahweh will bring about in accordance with
his plan. This idea culminated in the writings of the apocalypticists
who, believing history to be a preordained plot and divine drama,
sketched an overarching vision of history that culminates in the
divine judgment and glory. The Christian tradition developed its
vision of history according to the Hebraic idea, and included in the
chronology the concept of the messianic era anticipated by the
intertestamental writers. In the book of Revelation (chapter 20),
we read of this messianic age in the thousand-year reign of Christ,

commonly referred to as the Millennium. In the history of theology, different millenarian ideas are prominent in different periods and in different traditions. These different ideas have been broadly classified into three groups – premillennialism, postmillennialism and amillennialism. We shall examine each in turn.

Premillennialism

Premillennialism simply states that after the *parousia*, Christ will reign on earth for a thousand years before the final consummation of the kingdom of God in the new heavens and the new earth of the age to come.[8] At the second coming of Christ, the Antichrist will be judged and the righteous will be raised from the dead to reign with Christ in an era of peace and righteousness that will last a thousand years. After this period, Satan will be freed and will orchestrate a brief rebellion, which will be followed by the general resurrection, judgment and the eternal state. Revelation 19 – 22 is without doubt the *locus classicus* of premillenarian doctrine, because in these chapters the vision of the events of the *eschaton* (the end) is arranged in chronological order.[9] Also central to the interpretation of the premillennialists are the two resurrections Revelation 20 describes. Employing a literalist hermeneutics, all premillennialists argue that, taken in its most natural sense, these chapters in Revelation would lead to a premillenarian eschatology. 'Unless there is some reason intrinsic within the text itself which requires symbolic interpretation, or unless there are other Scriptures which interpret a parallel prophecy in a symbolic sense,' Ladd argues, 'we are required to employ a natural, literal interpretation.'[10]

Millenarian thought, which has a long history in Christian theology, is found in the writings of Justin Martyr and Irenaeus of Lyons. Combining the creation-day-age theory and the premillennialism of Papias and the Ephesian tradition, Justin postulates the seventh age of creation as the millennial era. Justin stoutly maintains that 'there will be a resurrection, and a thousand years in Jerusalem, which will then be built, adorned, and enlightened as the prophets and Ezekiel and Isaiah and others declare'. But at the same time, he is aware that other views prevail, and adds that 'many who belong to the pure and pious faith and are true Christians think otherwise'.[11] It was Irenaeus who offered the most complete presentation of the millennial vision in the patristic period in his polemic against the Gnostics, *Against Heresies*. It was also Irenaeus who presented a theological rationale for Christ's millennial reign: as the time of training in 'incorruption' for the righteous, to prepare them to inherit the spiritual kingdom and as recompense for their earthly suffering.[12] Modern premillennialists can be divided into two groups. The historic premillennialists, associated with scholars like G. E. Ladd, have tried to recover the millennial vision of the apocalyptic literature and the early church. These scholars reject dispensationalism but have sought to retain premillennialism with the resources of the patristic era. The second group, the dispensationalists, emerged in the closing decades of the nineteenth century in America and spread rapidly among the conservative and evangelical churches. Dispensationalism will be discussed in detail later in this chapter.

Critics often take issue with premillennialist hermeneutics, calling into question its literalism.[13] Amillennialists wonder if the premillennial vision is in full agreement with the broad teaching of the New Testament. These problems have to do not just with matters concerning chronology but also with significant theological issues. For instance, although premillennialists rightly emphasize the importance of the kingdom of God in eschatology, their understanding of the kingdom as the earthly rule of Christ during the Millennium has often been challenged.[14] The New Testament clearly teaches that the kingdom of God is already present and that its culmination will take place at the end of history and not within it. Furthermore, premillennialists understand the kingdom as a temporal reign that will last only for a limited time span, whereas the Bible clearly teaches that the kingdom is eternal. Equally problematic is the way in which the victory of Christ is envisioned by premillennialists. Why should believers be raised to inhabit an earth which is still not yet glorified? And why should the glorified Christ have to return to earth and rule over his enemies?[15] In other words, premillennialism creates serious theological anomalies by separating individual and cosmic eschatology. Finally, premillennialism actually contradicts the New Testament, which makes no mention of the 'third age' in which Christ will reign on earth.

Postmillennialism

In his book *The Millennium*, Loraine Boettner defines postmillennialism as 'that view of the last things which holds that the Kingdom of God is now being extended in the world through the preaching of the Gospel and the saving work of the Holy Spirit, that the world eventually will be Christianized, and that the return of Christ will occur at the close of the long period of righteousness and peace commonly called the Millennium'.[16] Although in some respects modern postmillennialism can be linked to the liberal movement, postmillennialists have often argued that this view can be traced to the patristic period. The turning point for the church in the Roman Empire came about when Constantine embraced the Christian faith and transformed the empire from 'the beast from the abyss' into the *imperium Christianum* (Christian empire), and Christianity into the dominant religion.[17] This period was quickly perceived as the thousand-year empire of Christ announced in Revelation 20 and the divine universal monarchy of Daniel 2 and 7. In similar vein, modern postmillennialists like Augustus Strong anticipate that a time will come when both Jews and Gentiles will become recipients of God's blessing of salvation, and Christianity will prevail throughout the earth.[18]

The golden age that postmillennialists expect to dawn in the future is different from that envisioned by the premillennialists because, unlike the latter, the former see the golden age not as that which Christ will inaugurate at his return but as the revolution in human society fostered by the gospel. Thus for postmillennialists the golden age signals the victory of the church in the world, the culmination of the age of the church. Some critics of postmillennialism have argued that the vision is flawed simply because it does not correspond to world events in the twentieth century. Such criticisms are weak because theology cannot simply be based on what happens in history or on the daily newspapers. The more theologically rigorous response is found in the criticism that postmillennialism, with its view of inexorable progress, simply fails to take into serious account the complex description of the end times found in the New Testament.[19] It fails to give cognizance to the fact that the New Testament's optimism is also always complemented by a pessimistic note (see, for example, Matthew 24:4–7; 2 Timothy 3:1–5). Furthermore the idea that in the end large numbers of people will be saved does not, according to critics, square with the biblical description. While rejecting universalism, postmillennialists envisage that nearly all human beings will put their faith in Christ because of their optimism in the power of the gospel. Critics respond by pointing out that Jesus indicated that the number of people who will be saved will be relatively small (Matthew 7:14).[20] Such optimism might seem justified in the case of China, for instance, where the number of people believing in Christ cannot be calculated with any great accuracy. But it can be confidently claimed that the church there has grown tenfold since 1949.

Amillennialism

Louis Berkhof has succinctly defined amillennialism as the doctrine which maintains 'that the present dispensation of the Kingdom of God will be followed immediately by the Kingdom of God in its consummate and eternal form'.[21] Amillennialists are not entirely satisfied with the term – which means 'no Millennium' – because it seems to suggest that this view ignores Revelation 20:1–6. This, however, is not the case. Amillennialism maintains that when Christ returns, he will judge the world and bring a decisive culmination of all things, including this present world. At his return, the dead will be raised, judged and assigned to their eternal destinies – the wicked to eternal punishment in hell, and the righteous to an eternal life of blessedness in the new heavens and the new earth. Amillennialism does not ignore Revelation 20:1–6 but interprets it not as a literal earthly reign of Christ prior to judgment but as an age beyond time when the kingdom of God is fully consummated. In my view, amillennialism best presents the New Testament eschatological vision.

Like premillennialists, amillennialists stress the priority of the New Testament over the Old, arguing that it is the New that interprets the Old. This led to the notion of the church as the 'spiritual Israel', since, according to amillennialist scholars, Scripture itself uses 'Israel' in both literal and figurative senses. The true Israelite is not merely a physical descendant of the patriarchs but is a person who has a right relationship with God (Genesis 32:28; Psalms 73:1; 125:5). The true Israel therefore are the new people of God, consisting of persons who have been regenerated by the Holy Spirit regardless of their ethnicity (Romans 2:28–29; 9:6–7; Galatians 3:29; 6:16; Philippians 3:3). The significance of the hermeneutical principle of the priority of the New Testament is that the promises originally given to Israel are fulfilled in the church. Stanley Grenz explains:

> The priority of the New Testament is crucial in the amillennial system. The employment of this principle results in the elimination of the necessity of a millennium. No future golden age is required for God to fulfill his promises to Israel. All promises to the nation either were already fulfilled in the Old Testament era or are being fulfilled during the church age, whether to the church or to the remnant of Israel.[22]

Amillennialists point out that throughout the New Testament a simple eschatological chronology is presented and insist that the millennial vision must be shaped by such a chronology (see 2 Peter 3:10–13). This present age will end with the return of the Lord in triumph to judge the righteous and the wicked and this will immediately be followed by the inauguration of the eternal states. Revelation 20 must therefore be interpreted within the framework of the general eschatological chronology of the New Testament and can neither supersede or contradict the general picture. Consequently, Revelation 20 is interpreted as a symbolic commentary of the Great Commission; that is, as referring to the present age between the two advents of Christ and not some future.[23] The 'thousand year reign' must not be interpreted literally but merely serves as an expression for a complete period of indeterminate length. Amillennialists take it to refer to the period 'that spans the entire New Testament dispensation, from the time of the first coming of Christ to just before the time of Christ's Second Coming'.[24] Unlike premillennialists who maintain that there are two resurrections – first that of the righteous and then that of the wicked – amillennialists insist that there is one general resurrection of both the righteous and the wicked for judgment at the end. And unlike dispensationalists who teach that Christ's return will take place in two phases – sometimes distinguished as *parousia* and revelation – that will be separated by a seven-year period, amillennialists maintain that Christ's return will be a single event.

Dispensationalism

In most fundamentalist churches and in some sectors of evangelicalism, an approach called 'dispensationalism', a variety of premillennialism, has in the twentieth century exerted a strong influence. Dispensationalism derives its name from the word 'dispensation', which is used in the Authorized Version of the Bible to refer to the administration of the household of God. Dispensationalists divide the history of the world into various epochs or eras to describe the economy of God in order that the different divine administrations of the affairs of the world may be distinguished. This movement, which dates from the early to mid-nineteenth century, receives its inspiration from the writings of J. N. Darby, one of the founders of the Plymouth Brethren. But it was the annotations of C. I. Scofield in the 1909 publication of an edition of the Authorized Version of the Bible, the Scofield

Reference Bible, that significantly helped to shape and spread dispensationalist ideas in America. In the 1960s, a new revised edition
called the New Scofield Bible was published, which retained the
earlier features of dispensationalist doctrine. One of the most
influential dispensationalist writers in America is Hal Lindsey, who
is most noted for his best-selling *The Late Great Planet Earth*, published by Zondervan in 1970.

An important feature of dispensationalism is its literalist
hermeneutics. Writers like Charles Ryrie maintain that the literal,
plain interpretation of the Bible is in line with the divine intention
for human language.[25] This method of interpretation must be
consistently applied throughout. To fail to do so is to lose all
objectivity in exegesis. While dispensationalists recognize the fact
that the Bible sometimes employs symbols, they maintain that
unless there are good contextual reasons for treating them as such,
they must be interpreted literally. The literalist hermeneutics that
dispensationalists employ is largely responsible for the way in
which they understand history and prophecy. This is clearly seen
in the way in which dispensationalists understand the future of
Israel in the light of Old Testament prophecies. Accusing conservative exegetes of inconsistency, dispensationalist scholars insist
that the prophecies concerning Israel must be fulfilled as they
were originally given. This means that Israel as a nation must
someday gain possession of the land of Palestine and enjoy all the
physical blessings mentioned in the Old Testament.[26]

Another feature of dispensationalism is the way in which it
periodizes salvation history into several epochs or dispensations.
There are seven dispensations: (1) paradise (human existence
before the fall, Genesis 1 – 3); (2) human rebellion (from the fall
to the flood, Genesis 3 – 7); (3) human authority (from the flood to
the call of Abraham, Genesis 8 – 11); (4) the patriarchal promise to
faith (from the call of Abraham to the ministry of Moses, Genesis
12 – Exodus 19); (5) law (from Moses to the coming of Christ,
Exodus 19 – Malachi); (6) grace or the church (first coming of
Christ to his return, Matthew 1 – Revelation 19); (7) millennial

kingdom (from the return of Christ to the final states, Revelation 20:2–15).[27] Although from as early as the patristic era theologians have schematized the history of the world, chiefly by using the six days of creation, Darby and Scofield introduced a schema that is clearly unprecedented. Stanley Grenz argues, however, that although the periodization of history is an important feature, the essence of dispensationalism lies in its dual concern – the relationship between Israel and the church, on the one hand, and the close of this age and the age to come, on the other.[28]

Many dispensationalists teach that the end of the period of grace and the perfecting of the cosmos will take place in two stages. The first is the rapture of the church. Christ will return in the air for his saints – both living and dead – who will be caught up with him in the air (John 14:3; 1 Corinthians 15:51–52; 1 Thessalonians 4:13–14). Some speak of a 'secret rapture', believing that this event will not be visible to non-believers. The rapture will be followed by a period of seven years during which the Holy Spirit will be absent. The gospel of the kingdom, however, will continue to be preached, although this is done not by the church but by those who came to faith due to the church's disappearance. Jews will play a significant role during this period, and the people of God will encounter the most severe persecution. This view is commonly termed 'pretribulationism', because it teaches that the church is raptured *before* the tribulation. At the end of this period, Christ will return to earth once again, this time *with* and not *for* his saints. After this, the millennial reign of Christ will be established, the nations will be judged, and Satan will be bound for a thousand years. Dispensationalists teach that during this period, the temple will be rebuilt and sacrifices will be offered once again, although they are now offered as a memorial. At the end of the thousand years, Satan will be released briefly before he is finally cast into the bottomless pit. The wicked will be raised and judged, and the new heavens and the new earth will be established.

Dispensationalism does consist of a number of clear biblical elements. Its emphasis on the return of Christ revitalized this hope in a time when many in the church were tempted to marginalize or forget it. In the same way, this emphasis has brought a timely challenge to Christian discipleship, especially against the 'post-millennial' atmosphere of the late nineteenth and early twentieth century. Furthermore, as Bruce Milne has pointed out, many of the leading voices of dispensationalism are men of profound spiritual learning who have studied the Bible with great diligence.[29] All this not withstanding, critics find the proposals of the dispensationalists problematic. Many reject the literalist hermeneutics espoused by dispensationalist scholars because they deem such an approach to the Bible to be too simplistic. The insistence that the prophecies of the Old Testament must be literally fulfilled in Israel is also heavily criticized by non-dispensationalist scholars, who argue that the Bible itself militates against such a view. A clear instance of this is the fulfilment of Joel's prophecy (2:28ff.) on the day of Pentecost (Acts 2:15–21). Luke applies this prophecy to the church, not Israel.[30]

Theologians have also criticized the dispensationalist doctrine of the pretribulation rapture of the church. In his Olivet Discourse, Jesus speaks of the Great Tribulation and warns his disciples to remain vigilant lest they fall away. There is no hint in this entire discourse of the rapture of believers before the tribulation. Pretribulationists maintain that since there is no mention of the word 'church' in this passage, Jesus must be speaking about a Jewish sect and not the church. Furthermore, the Gospel of Matthew was written specifically for the Jews. In response, critics have argued that the word 'church' (*ekklēsia*) appears in Matthew only three times, and its absence in the Olivet Discourse does not show anything.[31] The same statements are also found in the Gospel of Mark, which was certainly not written with the Jews as its intended audience.

Another important text that dispensationalists employ to support their doctrine of the pretribulation rapture of believers is 2 Thessalonians 2:1–13. In this text, Paul speaks of the Lord coming for his saints after the apostasy and the appearance of the 'man of lawlessness'. Because dispensationalists maintain that the church or the Holy Spirit is responsible for restraining the lawless one, they see this text as referring to the rapture. Critics disagree with this interpretation, and accuse pretribulationists of unwarranted speculation. Paul, they argue, does not identify the restrainer. They further argue that the opening words of the chapter indicate clearly that the appearance of the Antichrist and the great tribulation will precede the rapture of the church.[32] The dispensationalists have no grounds for distinguishing the 'coming of the Lord in the air' and 'the Day of the Lord'. These two descriptions refer to the same event. The same can be said of 'the blessed hope' mentioned in Titus 2:13. Critics maintain that this phrase does not refer to the secret rapture according to the dispensationalists' interpretation, but to the Day of the Lord, the glorious appearing of Christ.[33]

Finally critics also reject the dispensationalist doctrine of the two-stage coming of Christ. We recall that dispensationalists generally speak of two comings of Christ: as 'coming *for* his saints' (the rapture) and as 'coming *with* his saints' (the return). To be sure, 1 Thessalonians 3:13 does speak of the coming of the Lord 'with all his holy ones'. In order to understand what this means, one must be attentive to the context. The Thessalonians wanted to know if believers who have already died will miss the joy of Christ's second coming. In 1 Thessalonians 4:13–18 (commonly seen as the main New Testament passage on the rapture) Paul addresses this concern by assuring the Thessalonians that believers who have died will not miss out when the *parousia* takes place. Paul says that the dead in Christ will rise first, and, together with those who are alive, they will meet the Lord in the air. There is no mention of a two-stage coming of Christ here, or anywhere else in the New Testament. The main problem with dispensationalism is that it tries to fit the biblical data into the Procrustean bed it has created. Bruce Milne writes:

> One of the most disturbing aspects of this whole scheme is precisely that
> it is a scheme. As a result of this approach the warm person-centred

religion of the Bible is overlaid by a theoretical, impersonal scheme of happenings and events. While very many dispensationalists are exceptions to the rule, one cannot but wonder at the effect of this kind of approach upon personal religion and personal attitudes.[34]

The new creation

The return of Christ will bring about the new heavens and earth. Our sinful world will be transformed into a glorious reality and creation will finally achieve its *telos*. The doctrine of the new creation that Scripture clearly teaches is important for our understanding of the nature of salvation and the life to come for two reasons. The doctrine helps us to see God's redemptive programme in its entirety; that is, it involves not only individuals or humanity but also the whole of creation. It shows that just as sin has a cosmic dimension and disrupts the created order, so God's salvation extends to the material world. The doctrine enables us to envision the nature of the life to come and is thus profoundly related to the doctrine of the bodily resurrection. Glorified believers do not spend eternity in some ethereal heaven as disembodied spirits. The doctrine of the resurrection emphasizes the fact that humans are embodied beings and that their existence in the life to come will continue to have a bodily character. The doctrine of the new creation emphasizes that in the age to come, God's creation will not be nullified but be perfected. As Dermot Lane has put it so well, the doctrine of the new creation emphasizes that 'there is no salvation without the participation of creation, no redemption that by-passes the world, no heaven without earth'.[35]

The doctrine of the new creation is important also because it helps us to understand the nature of Old Testament prophecy. Dispensationalists have often accused amillennialists of spiritualizing Old Testament prophecies either by insisting that they provide a spiritualized interpretation of the church or by maintaining that they are poetic pictures of heaven. Dispensational premillennialism interprets these prophecies in relation to the millennial reign of Christ before the close of the age. This view is articulated clearly by Charles Ryrie:

> If the prophecies of the Old Testament concerning the promises of the future to Abraham and David are to be literally fulfilled, then there must be a future period, the millennium, in which they are fulfilled, for the church is not now fulfilling them in any literal sense. In other words, the literal picture of Old Testament prophecies demands either a future fulfilment or a nonliteral fulfilment. If they are fulfilled in the future, then the only time left for that fulfilment is the millennium.[36]

Amillennialists reply by stressing that the eschatological character of these prophecies implies that they will be fulfilled in the new heavens and new earth and not in the Millennium. They are unconvinced that all these prophecies should be understood literally and insist that some of them are presented in figurative language.

Will the new creation be brought into being *ex nihilo* (out of nothing), or will it be a transformation of the present created order? Lutheran orthodoxy teaches that except for angels and humans, the cosmos will be burnt with fire and dissolved into nothingness. This teaching finds scriptural warrant in 2 Peter 3:12, but it is also the outcome of the mystical theology of Lutheran orthodoxy. According to this view, in the new age human beings will be absorbed into the beatific vision and will no longer require earthly mediations. In the same way, earthly environments are no longer necessary in the state of blessedness. Only human beings, created in the image of God, will receive the salvation of God. The rest of creation will simply be destroyed. As Jürgen Moltmann describes it, 'Blessedness consists solely in the eternal contemplation of God. Its place is heaven.'[37] In the seventeenth century, this view was developed by Quenstedt; and in the twentieth century, it was defended by Lutheran theologian Paul Althaus.

Both patristic and Calvinist theology see the new creation as the transformation of this present cosmos into the state of perfection. Just as there are seeds of eternal life in the individual, so too

the future perfection lies latent in the present world, despite the
destructive effects of sin. Consequently, the end of the world
cannot be annihilation and new creation but a transformation out
of transience to eternity. This is indicated by the verb Revelation
21:5 uses: 'I am *making* [not 'creating'] everything new.' The new
creation is therefore of a piece with the salvation of individual
Christians. Commenting on Revelation 21:5, Robert Mounce
writes, 'The transformation which Paul saw taking place in the
lives of believers (2 Corinthians 3:18; 4:16–18; 5:16–17) will have its
counterpart on a cosmic scale when a totally new order will
replace the old marred by sin.'[38] The new creation is therefore not
'creation out of nothing' (*creatio ex nihilo*) but a transfiguration and
perfecting of this cosmos. This demonstrates God's commitment
and faithfulness to the world he has created. God's faithfulness to
the creation is such that he will ensure that the creation will
achieve its *telos*, despite the disruption caused by the fall. He does
this not by destroying the cosmos and creating a new one, but by
transforming and bringing to perfection this present creation.

What will the new creation be like? A number of passages in
the Bible provide eloquent description of the new reality (chiefly,
Isaiah 65:17–25; 66:22–23; 2 Peter 3:13; Revelation 21:1–4). In Isaiah
65:17–20, we find the description of a reality that in some sense
mirrors the present reality, but without its frustrations and
sufferings. In the following chapter, Isaiah speaks of the permanent nature of the new heavens and the new earth: the Lord
will make them endure (66:22). The inhabitants of the new earth
will also be involved constantly in worship. 'What is predicted
here', Hoekema writes, 'is the perpetual worship of all the people
of God, gathered from all nations, in ways which will be suitable
to the glorious new existence they will enjoy on the new earth.'[39]
Peter replies to the scoffers by making the point that God will
bring about a new heaven and a new earth that will last for ever.
Everything sinful and imperfect will be removed. Peter calls the
new creation 'the home of righteousness' (2 Peter 3:13). The
proper attitude is therefore not to scoff at the delays of the

promised events but eagerly to await the return of Christ, after which the transformation of the cosmos will take place.

Surely the most impressive and breathtaking description of the new creation is found in Revelation 21:1–4. These verses describe a glorious new reality, brought home by the word *kainos* (new): it is not a universe totally unlike the present one, which has been gloriously renewed. The church is described in verse 2 as the 'holy city, new Jerusalem' that will descend from heaven to earth, without spot or blemish, prepared and ready for the marriage of the Lamb (see Revelation 19:7). The earth itself will be the dwelling place of God, and this implies that in the new creation, heaven and earth will no longer be separated but will merge. Verse 4 shows how life in the new creation is qualitatively different from life in this present world, which is marked by suffering and pain: 'He will wipe every tear from their eyes. There will be no more death or mourning or crying or pain, for the old order of things has passed away' Revelation 21:4). Hans Schwarz is right when he comments that 'it is next to impossible to say anything meaningful [about the new creation] without indulging in speculations'.[40] Eternal blessing, writes Robert Mounce, 'is couched in negation because the new and glorious order is more easily pictured in terms of what it replaces than by an attempt to describe what is largely inconceivable in our present state'.[41] What is clear from the description is that the old order, marred by sin and corruption, will give way to a new order characterized by perfection, harmony and blessedness.

8

LIVING IN HOPE

The ground of hope

In the preceding chapters I have constructed a Christian eschatology, but in this chapter, I reflect on the implications of biblical hope on Christian existence in the world. It should be clear from the exposition in the previous chapters that Christian hope is profoundly different – even antithetical – to secular expressions of progress and optimism. Christian hope is not founded upon self-confidence or confidence in the human race. Rather Christian hope is established in God, who, through his Word, has promised the renewal and perfection of humankind and the creation. The profound and inextricable relationship between hope and faith is thus paramount. Because it is so rooted in God, Christian hope must always possess that quality of transcendence. As an expression of faith, which is interpreted here as trust, Christian hope transcends our present circumstances and experience and is anchored in the promises of God in Christ. As such, we should be wary of those philosophies and sciences that claim to explain everything, or that seek to unify life and render everything clear and certain. Such claims signal the loss of transcendence, without which hope in the theological sense cannot be understood.

For the Christian, God is never just the *object* of hope but is also the *basis* of hope. Put differently, the Christian not only hopes *for* God but *in* God. It is therefore not enough to claim that God or transcendence is the *ground* of Christian hope. Theologies that speak abstractly of God as the 'Absolute' or as 'Being-in-itself' or as the 'Ground of Being' are often in danger of distorting the concept of God altogether. It is not sufficient to focus merely on the ultimate, indefeasible nature of transcendence; one must also be concerned with its deeply and fully personal character. And this can be known only through God's self-disclosure in Jesus Christ, his incarnate Word. In Jesus Christ, we come to know that God is with us and for us. In the incarnate Word is revealed the essence of God as Trinity – as the communion of Father, Son and Holy Spirit – and hence also man's communal destiny. Christian hope is not just in God, but in God's final reordering of the whole of creation, redeeming it from the perversions of sin, and transforming it to perfection. Human relationships will be ordered under the standard of love. As Glenn Tinder has put it, 'The end of the ages must bring a community as deep and immutable as God himself in the perfect life and vitality of the Holy Trinity.'[1]

In this way, Christian hope distinguishes itself from philosophical and religious teleologies: it is not established on the basis of a general metaphysics or understanding of history, but on the revelation of God's will for the world in Jesus Christ. For Christians, Christ is the axis of history; that is, in Christ, history has its origins as well as its climax. In Christ is to be found the answers to the questions human beings have been asking, in him is the fulfilment of their efforts to reach transcendence through their intellect and imagination. As Brunner puts it, 'Through this unity of faith and hope the revelation of the inscrutable will of God in Jesus Christ becomes the answer to man's deeply felt question as to the meaning of his existence; an answer which he himself is not capable of providing.'[2] Furthermore, because fallen human beings are not so clear-sighted that they are able always to ask the right questions, God's revelation in Christ not only provides answers but also directs the questions. And, insofar as human beings are unable to anticipate the answers, the revelation of God is bound to be surprising and unforeseen. Illustrative of this is the fact that for the Christian faith, the salvation of humankind is bound up with the death of a Jew on the cross, a death that took place at the remote outskirts of Graeco-Roman Jerusalem some two thousand years ago.

The Sermon on the Mount, which is a word of hope, shows that Christian hope is not just about a future reality but is one mysteriously hidden in the present.[3] This is because the Sermon's central figure, Christ, has already come into the world and has inaugurated the divine kingdom; and insofar as we are united with him we are capable of fellowship with God. The hope of salvation, of eternal life, is therefore not merely a future utopia, a vision of an ideal that does not exist. Rather eternal life is *real* life, which exists even in the here and now for those who are in communion with Jesus Christ. This is expressed by Paul, who confidently proclaims that the salvation of believers is not just a future reality but one already appropriated by believers in the here and now: 'For in this hope we *were* saved' (Romans 8:24, my emphasis). Paul uses the aorist to bring out the nature of Christian hope,[4] to emphasize the confidence in the purpose and power of God, and to show that the future salvation that Christians hope for is in some sense already a present reality. To be sure, true hope is indefeasible because it is anchored in eternity. And temporal events are significant, not in themselves, but only in relation to eternity. Yet that for which we hope lies not merely in the future, but is already present now, albeit not in full measure. Because the eternal Word of God has become flesh, eternity has penetrated human history, and the kingdom of God has been inaugurated.

Worship and hope

The central activity of the eschatological community, the church, is worship. The New Testament uses a variety of terms to describe this activity, which enable us to understand its different aspects better. The most common term, *latreia*, which is simply translated 'worship', is used to refer to Jewish worship in the temple (Hebrews 9:1, 6) or religious duty (John 16:2). The word is also sometimes translated as service. *Proskynein* refers to falling down to show obeisance. It is used by Jesus when he tells the Samaritan woman that a time will come when 'true worshippers will worship the Father in spirit and truth' (John 4:23). The physical aspect of worship is underscored by this verb. *Thysia*, which means 'sacrifice', is used several times to describe Christian worship (Romans 12:1; Hebrews 13:15). And *prosphora*, 'offering', is used in relation to the body of Christ, which was offered once and for all (Hebrews 10:10). Both these words play a significant role in the development of the theology of the Eucharist. Together these metaphors bring colour to the monochromic English word 'worship'.

Central to our theme is the relationship between the church's worship and time. In worship, the church achieves a different perspective of time and history from that which the world operates. Because Jesus Christ is the beginning and end, the church understands time and history in the light of the *telos* of the creation. Furthermore, because the church understands worship as an eschatological event, her concept of time is multitextured. The church understands time as more than *chronos* (a period of time) because the revelation of God in Jesus Christ emphasizes that in the incarnation, eternity has entered history. The presence of eternity in human history means that the notion of past, present and future is blurred. This is exemplified in the church's commemoration of Good Friday and in her celebration of Easter. These special celebrations not only recall what God has done through Christ for the salvation of humankind, but also anticipate the consummation of his kingdom. In these events, the church celebrates the future that is already here even as she anticipates its fullness. In this way, worship that takes place in time not only reveals the meaning of time but also renews and gives it meaning.[5]

As worship gives witness to *kairos* (a point in time) that is at odds with *chronos*, it serves as a sign of the end. The worship of the church therefore witnesses to the end of history and the coming into being of the new heavens and the new earth. All things that have to do with the worship of the church – Scripture, hymns, prayers, sacraments, proclamation – contain manifold promises of the end. In this sense, the eschatological community, the church, gives witness to a different future than the one envisioned by human society. This eschatological perspective means that the best of human achievement and the most remarkable progress human society has witnessed must be understood at best as penultimate. Ecclesiology can never be separated from eschatology. The church exists in both *chronos* and *kairos*, in temporality as well as in God-filled time. Through her worship, the church gains insight into her own identity as an eschatological community; that is, as a community that lives within a creation (not merely a cosmos) that is a graced horizon, one shot through with the active presence of the Creator.[6] The church bears witness to this saving activity of God even as she awaits the consummation of the divine kingdom.

Worship enables the church to get occasional glimpses of the *eschaton* in the course of her temporal journey in this world. Worship enables Christians to discern the glimmering of heaven, as it were, in the ordinary and even mundane events of life. Hope gives us the capacity to see acts of bravery or love in this temporal world as 'eschatological moments'; that is, as glimpses – however momentary – of the glory to come. And in this sense, the hope that worship nourishes enables us to discern the meaning and value of our existence better, even in the face of apparent meaninglessness and futility. In the next section, I shall discuss the problem of suffering in the light of hope. What is of moment here is that the eschatological character of worship enables Christians to get glimpses of 'eschatological moments', and therefore to hope. As Tinder has so eloquently put it, 'Where there is hope, the splendour of earthly things – of light, of firmament, of sea and land, of sun, moon and stars – are not transient glories but are analogues of God and the heavenly company which is destined finally to be as visible and present as mountains and trees are now.'[7]

As eschatological activity, worship opens us to the natural 'sacramentality' of the world in which we live. By participating in this activity, the church is able to perceive the depth of meaning embedded in the realities of this world. This is because in worship the church realizes that the story of our world is caught up in the story of the cross and resurrection of Christ. Thus while the church lives very much in this world, it speaks the language of sacrament and icon until the return of Christ. The worldliness of worship reminds us of the significance of the world God has created even as it enables us to understand its true meaning.

This brings us to the sacraments of the church, baptism and the Eucharist. In the New Testament, baptism is always placed in an eschatological context, as it signifies entrance into the kingdom of God. Although the meanings of baptism are multilayered and have been developed differently throughout the history of the church, James White identifies five metaphors that can be gleaned from the New Testament presentation.[8] The first is union with Jesus Christ. Baptism conveys to the baptized the death of Christ and the possibility of resurrection (Romans 6:3–5; Colossians 2:12). The second is incorporation into the body of Christ, the church. This is clearly articulated by Paul, who wrote in his letter to the Galatians, 'for all of you who were baptised into Christ have clothed yourselves with Christ. There is neither Jew nor Greek, slave nor free, male nor female, for you are all one in Christ Jesus' (3:27–28; see also 1 Corinthians 12:13). The third metaphor is new birth or regeneration (*palingenesia*), which is closely tied to the first metaphor. Baptism is therefore referred to as both womb and tomb. Fourthly there is the metaphor of the forgiveness of sins. In Acts, the relationship between baptism and forgiveness of sins is made clear in Peter's sermon: 'Repent and be baptised, every one of you, in the name of Jesus Christ for the forgiveness of your

sins' (Acts 2:38a). The final metaphor, the reception of the Holy
Spirit, is found in Acts 2:38b. All these metaphors have an eschatological character – they describe realities that have already dawned
upon humankind but that await fulfilment in the future – and thus
are signs of hope.

Traditionally, the Eucharist is held as the queen of the sacraments. The imagery of the Eucharist as a sacred meal can be traced
to the Old Testament, particularly at the making of the covenant
with Moses on Mount Sinai (Exodus 24:9–11). In the description of
the Eucharist in the New Testament as the 'cup of the new
covenant', we hear echoes of Exodus 24, which gives an account of
the covenant with Moses. This meal imagery is found in the
wisdom literature and famously in Psalm 23:5, where the divine
providence and fellowship is described with the use of this imagery:

> You prepare a table before me
>   in the presence of my enemies.
> You anoint my head with oil;
>   my cup overflows.

In the writings of the prophets, the meal imagery is used to refer
to the eschatological messianic banquet. Thus in the Isaianic
apocalypse we read:

> On this mountain the LORD Almighty will prepare
>   a feast of rich food for all peoples,
> a banquet of aged wine –
>   the best of meats and the finest of wines.
>   (Isaiah 25:6)

In instituting the Eucharist, Jesus draws these various strands of the
tradition into the meal he shared with his disciples before his brutal
execution. More importantly, by this meal Jesus signals the beginning of a new covenant God is making with his people through his
death and resurrection. Geoffrey Wainwright comments:

We may therefore confidently suppose that in the time of Jesus the Jews looked for the coming of the Messiah in the same night as that in which the great deliverance from Egypt had been wrought. This messianic expectation would then mark the meal during which, according to the synoptic gospels, Jesus instituted the Eucharist.[9]

Wainwright delineates some important features of the Eucharist in his book. The Eucharist as an eschatological sign expresses both continuity and discontinuity, thereby bringing together the past, present and future of the reign of God, the earthly meal as well as the heavenly banquet. The Eucharist employs ordinary gifts of food and drink, bread and wine, 'the structures of reality', thus emphasizing our profound dependence on the Creator. It exploits incarnational Christology to the fullest: 'Christ is food, table companion and host.'[10] Further, the Eucharist transcends the dualism of the material and the spiritual by pointing, on the one hand, to the eternal purposes of God, and, on the other, by emphasizing that it is in the material world that his purposes will be fulfilled. And finally, the Eucharist enables us to understand the communal nature of the reign of God. Like every aspect of the worship of the church, the sacraments sketch the vision of the future. They enable us to 'remember the future', to quote Rebecca Kuiken's delightful and profound expression.[11]

Evil, suffering and hope

The universal problem of evil and suffering has not only presented a serious challenge to the secular idea of progress but also to Christian theism. As we have seen, the phenomenal progress in science and technology has not only failed to eradicate evil in the world but has in some ways perpetuated it. In the modern world, the problem of evil is a challenge to theism, especially Christian theism with its concept of a sovereign and good God. Theologians like Michael Buckley,[12] Kenneth Surin[13] and Terrence Tilley[14] have convincingly demonstrated the profound link between modern

theodicies and the Enlightenment. To be sure, the early fathers of
the church were also profoundly aware of the problem the existence of evil poses to Christian theism. But they did not consider
the existence of evil to be the *ultimate* challenge to belief in God in
the way post-Enlightenment thinkers do. Kenneth Surin explains:

> Pre-seventeenth century Christian thinkers were certainly not unaware
> of the conceptual difficulties that these antinomies [between divine
> omnipotence and worldly evils] generated; but, unlike their post-
> seventeenth century counterparts, they did not regard these problems
> as constituting any sort of ground for jettisoning their faith.[15]

Be that as it may, the problem of evil does present a conceptual
challenge to anyone who wishes to take faith in God seriously.
And reflection on the future of the world with God must deal
with the problem of the ubiquity of evil in the present and also
with the question pertaining to evil's future.

The Bible offers no clear answers to the question of the origin
of evil. The theories hitherto put forward – that evil is an initial
component of existence, that it is a price that must be paid for the
sake of cosmic harmony – are not only unconvincing but fly in the
face of the scriptural testimony. The opening chapters of Genesis
tell us that when God had finished his work of creation on the
sixth day, he rejoiced to behold a creation that was 'very good'.
The world made 'by God, through God and for God' did not
contain even the embryonic presence of evil.[16] But if God created
the world to be an expression of goodness, whence evil? Although
the Bible does not answer this question directly, it does establish a
profound link between the fall and the entrance of evil into the
world. This includes what has been traditionally – and inade-
quately – dubbed as 'natural evil', which, according to the biblical
presentation, are disruptions introduced to the created order by
the primeval fall. This view is highly unpopular in modern theology, not least due to the pervasive influence of the theory of
evolution. But as Gunton puts it when commenting on the fall,

we cannot escape its implications that in some way or other the created order suffered a primal catastrophe of cosmic proportions and that human sin – a disrupted relation with the creator – is in some way constitutive of it.[17]

Alongside the problem of evil and theodicy is the problem of suffering. The ethic of the cross exclusive to the Christian faith has enabled Christians to embrace suffering creatively and to see it in the light of God's redemptive grace. Christian realism towards suffering therefore stands at the extreme opposite side of the spectrum to accounts found in religions like Hinduism, which understand suffering as illusory and hence deny its reality. Only in the light of the cross of Christ can Christians learn to delight in their infirmities and be content with weaknesses, insults, hardships, persecutions and difficulties (2 Corinthians 12:10). The Christian understands that faith in the cross requires *participation* in the cross. And when undertaken willingly as participation in the crucifixion of Christ, suffering itself takes on new meaning and is mysteriously redirected by grace to bring spiritual benefits to the sufferer. 'Suffering becomes, in a manner of speaking, ecstatic – not in mood, but in raising us out of a degraded past and above a degraded self.'[18]

But, as the apostle Paul makes clear, Christian realism possesses an even greater depth, since its scope of vision stretches beyond the present reality and encompasses the promised redemption: the future glory. Paul thus deals with the problem of suffering eschatologically, not just from the perspective of individual salvation but also from that of cosmic transformation: 'I consider that our present sufferings are not worth comparing with the glory that will be revealed in us' (Romans 8:18). In the light of the certainty of this redemption, Paul appeals to Christians to exercise patient hope (Romans 8:24–25) in the wake of the troubles of life in this fallen reality. The problems of evil and suffering cannot be solved philosophically but only theologically and eschatologically; that is, in the light of what God has accomplished in the cross of Christ and what he will bring about in the fullness of time.

Such a 'solution' to the difficult problems of evil and suffering in the world will surely not satisfy some. Fyodor Dostoevsky in *The Brothers Karamazov* (Part 2, Book 5, Chapter 4) has given voice to this objection through the figure of Ivan Karamazov. During a visit to his brother Aloysha at the monastery, the atheist Ivan reveals his inability to accept God's world because of the universal presence of evil and suffering. He lists the atrocities he has seen and experienced: the lashing of a worn-out horse by a drunk, a baby brutally murdered in front of his mother by marauding Turks, and a boy torn to pieces by hounds because he accidentally injured a general's hound at play. Ivan confesses that he cannot understand why things should be thus ordered. He does not accept the idea that everything will be worked out when the grand purpose of God is in the end accomplished, and asks if even such a divine purpose is worth the tears of one tortured child. 'It isn't God I don't accept, Aloysha,' he insists, denying his atheism, 'it's just his ticket that I most respectfully return to him.' He ends with this famous challenge to his brother:

> 'Tell me yourself, I challenge you – answer. Imagine that you are creating a fabric of human destiny with the object of making men happy in the end, giving them peace and rest at last, but that it was essential and inevitable to torture to death one tiny creature – that baby beating its breast with its fist, for instance – and founded that edifice on its unavenged tears, would you consent to be the architect on those conditions? Tell me, and tell the truth.'
>
> 'No, I wouldn't consent', said Aloysha softly.[19]

Ivan's approach is representative of many modern theodicies. The argument is based on a certain preconceived premise; namely that a sovereign and good God *must* create a world that excludes the possibility of evil. This presupposition is then used against the existence of God in favour of atheism by a circular argument. Since God – if he truly exists – must create a world without the possibility of evil, and since evil does exist, God therefore does not exist. This line of thought is only possible because the acids of secularism have already eaten away the fabric of faith. As Wolfhart Pannenberg has so perceptively put it:

> So long as faith in God the Creator holds firm, the question of theodicy can be no real threat to it because this faith also carries with it the conviction that God and his counsels are above all creaturely understanding. Only when we deal with the existence of the Creator as a debatable postulate that we have to support by argument does the problem of theodicy carry a weight that can easily tip the scales in favour of atheism.[20]

Put differently, only when God is seen as nothing other than a hypothesis that can be challenged does the problem of theodicy become acute. This is a restatement of my earlier observation regarding the relationship between Enlightenment rationalism and theodicy.

As we have seen in the discussion in previous chapters, the eschatological coming of God will bring about the transformation of this world of sin and death into the glorious new heavens and new earth in which evil will have no place. 'In all its forms and individual themes biblical eschatology has to do with the over-coming of wickedness and evil.'[21] The New Testament indicates that the irrational force of evil can be understood only in its defeat by the life, death, resurrection and ascension of Jesus Christ. In the incarnation, Jesus Christ made manifest the character of evil as the enemy of the created order by taking on human flesh and bearing the effects of evil in it in order to destroy it. The problem with many 'theodicies' is that they try to explain the inexplicable and seek to tame the problem of evil without appealing to the incarna-tion and the cross. The defeat of evil through the cross of Christ means that God has chosen to eradicate evil eschatologically. Evil will be destroyed in God's 'good time' just as God takes his time in perfecting the creation.[22] That destruction and overcoming, however, is already anticipated in the cross and resurrection of

Christ and in the giving of the Holy Spirit. By the cross, God profoundly turned evil against itself.[23] In the cross, evil is conquered
as evil in that the supreme crime, the murder of the only righteous
man, becomes the basis for the abolition of sin. In this 'sin of sins',
the murder of the incarnate Son, the greatest love is demonstrated
and the wages earned by man's sin is borne. In the cross, God's
justice – that evil be punished – is met by his love, in the giving of
his Son, innocent of sin, to take the place of the guilty vicariously.

The presence of evil in the world 'between the times', that is,
between the first and second advents of Christ, points to the
unfathomable mystery of God's plan. The uneasy entanglement
of the 'already' and the 'not yet' of the kingdom (discussed in an
earlier chapter), their striving against each other in confusion, is
characteristic of our world that awaits the consummation of the
kingdom. The first coming of the kingdom signals the suppres-
sion of evil but not its destruction. The first coming mysteriously
embraces evil while the will of God is carried out, while the
second coming destroys evil completely as the divine will is
fulfilled. Evil, defined in the Bible as resistance to the divine will,
will be destroyed once that will is fully realized at the consummation of God's reign. Only the eyes of faith will be able to penetrate
the ambiguities, tensions and chaos of the present reality and perceive the mystery of the divine purpose. To the martyrs who cry
'How long?', the reply is given that the number of the elect is to be
completed first (Revelation 6:11). Before the end comes, the good
news must be preached to all the nations (Mark 13:10), because
God desires all people to be saved (1 Timothy 2:6). God in his
patience allows himself to appear negligent with respect to his
promises in order that all may come to repentance (2 Peter 3:9).
But already with the first advent of Christ and the inauguration of
the divine kingdom we see a foretaste, which carries with it access
to the future consummation. 'God' Pannenberg maintains,

> anticipates his own eschatological vanquishing of wickedness and evil by
> his entering our creaturely time that brings about his future victory over

evil and the deliverance of his creatures inasmuch as this divine
anticipation gives them the chance as creatures, after the overcoming of
their alienation from God, to acquire a share in his coming kingdom.[24]

But before the end comes, the tension remains. In his book
Theology of the Pain of God, the Japanese theologian, Kazoh
Kitamori, describes it as follows:

> The tension arising from the fusion of these two contradictory truths is
> eschatological in the deepest sense of the word. The answer to this
> insolvable contradiction can only be sought in hope. The tension which
> faith holds continues on with the hope for a final vindication at the end
> of the world. The faith living in this reality – the resolved within the
> unresolved – is truly eschatological. Inasmuch as this structure is basic to
> the gospel, the eschatological content is also basic to the gospel.[25]

Hope and discipleship

Finally we turn to the subject of discipleship, and ask how
Christian hope should influence the way we live in the world. This
question may be put differently: How does our hope in the
God who will bring all things to perfection influence our view of
the world in which we live and our role in it? Does the vision
of the transformed reality lead us somehow to place too little
value in this world? I have been discussing the need for transcendence, and the consequences the loss of transcendence has on our
perception of the world. We saw that the erosion of belief in transcendence has resulted in the growing concern with this world
for its own sake, and that this is seen in every aspect of human
culture – science, economics, politics. Does the converse produce
the opposite result? Does other-worldliness lead to this-worldly
indifference? Some may argue that Paul seems to lean in this direc-
tion when he insists that for believers it is preferable to be away
from the body and at home with the Lord (2 Corinthians 5:6, 8).
Christians, of course, place more importance on this world than

Hindus, whose concept of *maya* leads them to the conclusion that this-worldly reality is an illusion. Still, the belief that the future holds something better and something 'other' than the here and now has led some Christians to view this world as less important. A hymn by James Montgomery in the early nineteenth century hints at this perspective:

Here in the body pent,
Absent from Him I roam,
Yet nightly pitch my moving tent
A day's march nearer home.

My Father's house on high,
Home of my soul, how near
At times, to faith's foreseeing eye
Thy golden gates appear!

Ah, then my spirit faints
To reach the land I love,
The bright inheritance of saints,
Jerusalem above.

True hope, however, does not urge us to take flight of the present for the future, but enables us to face the present with all its suffering, pain and disappointment with profound realism. True hope enables us to live in the present and never allows us to leave the present for the future. Although Christian hope comprises a vision of the future, the *eschaton*, it nurtures a unique spirituality that strives in humility to be adequate to the circumstances God has placed us in. This means that true hope can never inspire an escapist outlook. When threatened by pain, sorrow and suffering, he who truly hopes does not immediately try to project himself into the future by imagining some utopia. Rather, he will with resolve face the vicissitudes of life by simply continuing to live his life before God. Cardinal John Henry Newman has expressed this with great poignancy and eloquence in his hymn 'Lead, Kindly Light, amid circling gloom'. Though 'the night is dark and I am far from home', yet he pleads that God would 'keep Thou my feet; I do not ask to see the distant scene, – one step enough for me'.[26]

In Asia, the idea of world denial and separation embodied either in Buddhist or Hindu mysticism is common, especially in countries like Thailand and India where the ubiquity of monumental monasteries and of holy men serves as its constant reminders. Christian hope, however, betokens a very different form of spirituality. Originating as it does from the ancient Hebrews, Christian hope, profoundly rooted in history, believes that God is the sovereign creator of space and time. The same observation may be made when Christian hope and the vision of the Greeks are compared. The Greeks see the world as mere reflections of some eternal order. Jews and Christians see the heavens as the 'new heavens and new earth', a new creation in which the evils of this present age, the 'night' and the 'sea', are eradicated. As Tinder puts it, 'such images, drawn from Jewish apocalypse and from the New Testament, suggest how radically different an ontology compared with that of the Greeks, Christian hope rests on'.[27] Because it is so rooted in history, Christian hope envisages the story of humankind, not just our personal stories, as part of God's story, a story fashioned by the sovereign and merciful God.

This brings us to the relationship between Christian hope and the cross. We have seen in previous chapters that Christian hope is profoundly shaped by the cross of Christ. Through the cross we come to understand that the worst events can be meaningful and that disappointments and tribulations are part of the course of life in the fallen world. But the cross also enables us to see that every disappointment and suffering we now face can be integrated into the story God fashions, which will ultimately serve our welfare. The dialectic of the cross means that hope is both prepared for disappointments here and is sure of eternity in the age to come. The cross and the resurrection of Christ reveal the dialectical nature of hope itself. Hope is dialectical simply because the present conditions are antithetical to those for which we hope. We hope for righteousness in the midst of moral degradation, for justice in the midst of injustice and oppression, and for life in the midst of death. 'In the dialectic of destiny, we confront our folly, sinfulness, weakness, and mortality, and in doing this we also confront, through grace, the wisdom, and righteousness, and power, and everlasting God.'[28]

As a life of hope, the Christian life is therefore lived expectantly. Jesus stresses this when he exhorts his disciples to 'keep watch, because you do not know the day or the hour' (Matthew 25:13). This emphasis should not be read as an injunction for the disciples to withdraw from the world in order to prepare themselves 'spiritually' for his return. Neither does it encourage a fascination for the signs of the end and a misplaced preoccupation with speculating about the date of the *parousia*. Rather Jesus' teaching is purposed to point out that the preparations the disciples must make are essentially of a this-worldly nature, for the presence of the new creation is already hidden in the form of the old. And it can be recognized 'not in mystical fervour or some purifying detachment from the world, but precisely in radical involvement in the world through purifying it through initiatives for divine justice, peace and the life to which these lead'.[29] The church, to be sure, is not of this world; yet it is called to be in the world and to value the world in the light of its future. This calling is not an optional extra, but is that of every follower of Jesus Christ.

NOTES

1. HOPE IN ASIA

1 Glenn Tinder, *The Fabric of Hope* (Scholars Press, 1999), p. 14.

2 Gabriel Marcel, 'Sketch of a Phenomenology and a Metaphysic of Hope', *Homo Viator: Introduction to a Metaphysics of Hope*, translated by Emma Graufurd (Gollancz, 1951), p. 36.

3 Anthony Giddens, *The Consequences of Modernity* (Polity, 1990), p. 6.

4 Patricia Crone, *Pre-Industrial Societies* (Blackwell, 1989), p. 196.

5 Ibid., pp. 196–197.

6 Andrew Tan, 'The Indigenous Roots of Conflict in Southeast Asia: The Case of Mindanao', in Kumar Ramakrishna and See Seng Tan (eds.) *After Bali: The Threat of Terrorism in Southeast Asia* (Institute of Defence and Strategic Studies, 2003), p. 97.

7 Rohan Gunaratna, 'Understanding Al Qaeda and its Network in Southeast Asia', in Ramakrishna and Seng, *After Bali*, p. 125.

8 Daljit Singh, 'ASEAN Counter-Terror Strategies and Cooperation: How Effective?', in Ramakrishna and Seng, *After Bali*, p. 211.

9 Jürgen Moltmann, 'Hope in a Time of Arrogance and Terror', in Jon L. Berquist (ed.), *Strike Terror No More: Theology, Ethics and the New War* (Chalice, 2002), p. 185.

10 Ibid., p. 184.

11 Ronald Hill, *Southeast Asia: People, Land and Economy* (Allen & Unwin, 2002), p. 138.

12 Randolf David, 'Asian Societies in the Age of Globalisation', *Faith and Life in Contemporary Asian Realities* (Christian Conference of Asia, 2000), p. 23.

13 Richard Robison and David S. G. Goodman, 'The New Rich in Asia: Economic Development, Social Status and Political Consciousness', in Richard Robison and David S. G. Goodman (eds.), *The New Rich in Asia: Mobile Phones, McDonald's and Middle-Class Revolution* (Routledge, 1996), p. 7.

14 'Message to the Asian Communities: Final Statement of the Kandy Conference', *Dialogue* 7 (September–December 1980), p. 119.

15 Gunnar Myrdall, *Asian Drama: An Inquiry into the Poverty of Nations*, 3 vols. (Allen Lane, 1968).

16 A. A. Yewangoe, *Theologia Crucis in Asia* (Rodopoli, 1987), p. 11.

17 Dewi Hughes and Matthew Bennett, *God of the Poor: A Biblical Vision of God's Present Rule* (OM, 1998), p. 162.

18 Hans Küng, 'Toward Dialogue', in Hans Küng, Josef Van Ess, Heinrich von Stietencron and Heinz Bechert, *Christianity and World Religions: Paths of Dialogue with Islam, Hinduism, and Buddhism* (SCM, 1993), p. xvii.

19 Translated by Narada Maha Thera (1980), *The Buddha and His Teachings* (Stamford Press charitable reprint, no date).

20 Paul Williams, *Buddhist Thought* (Routledge, 2000), p. 42.

21 R. Gethin, *The Foundations of Buddhism* (Oxford University Press, 1998).

22 Ibid.

23 Ibid., pp. 48–49.

24 Julius Lipner, *Hinduism: Their Religious Beliefs and Practices* (Routledge, 1994), p. 230.

25 Heinrich von Stietencron, 'Hindu Perspectives', in Küng, Van Ess, Stietencron and Bechert, *Christianity and World Religions*, pp. 217–218.

26 Brian Hebblethwaite, *Evil, Suffering and Religion* (SPCK, 2000), p. 58.

27 Cited in Maurice Meisner, *Marxism, Maoism and Utopianism: Eight Essays* (University of Wisconsin Press, 1982), p. 165.

28 Donald MacInnis, *Religious Policy and Practice in Communist China: A Documentary History* (Macmillan, 1972), p. 60.

29 Mao Zedong, 'The Chinese Revolution and the Chinese Communist Party' (December 1939), in *Selected Works of Mao Tse-tung*, vol. 2 (Foreign Language Press, 1975), pp. 306–307.

30 Mao Zedong, 'The Foolish Old Man Who Removed Mountains' (June 1945), in ibid., vol. 3, p. 322.

31 Paul Rule, 'Is Maoism Open to the Transcendent?', in Michael Chu (ed.), *The New China: A Catholic Response* (Paulist Press, 1977), p. 40.

32 Dermot A. Lane, *Keeping Hope Alive: Stirrings in Christian Theology* (Gill & Macmillan, 1996), p. 59.

33 Ibid., p. 60.

34 Emil Brunner, *Eternal Hope* (Lutterworth, 1954), p. 19.

35 Quoted in Richard Bauckham and Trevor Hart, *Hope against Hope: Christian Eschatology at the Turn of the Millennium* (Eerdmans, 1999), p. 5.

36 Tinder, *Fabric of Hope*, p. 15.

37 Ibid., p. 31.

38 Lane, *Keeping Hope Alive*, p. 69.

2. THE HOPE OF ISRAEL

1 James K. Hoffmeier, 'Plagues of Egypt', *New International Dictionary of Old Testament and Exegesis* (Zondervan, 1997), vol. 4, p. 1056.

2 Derek Kidner, *Genesis*, Tyndale Old Testament Commentaries (IVP, 1967), p. 46.

3 John Watts, *Isaiah 34–66*, Word Biblical Commentary (Word, 1987), p. 92.

4 Brevard Childs, *Isaiah*, Old Testament Library (SCM, 2001), p. 311.

5 Claus Westermann, *Isaiah 40–66*, Old Testament Library (SCM, 1969), p. 140.

6 Walter Brueggemann, *1 & 2 Kings* (Smyth & Helwys, 2000), p. 508.

7 Marvin Tate, *Psalms 51–100*, Word Biblical Commentary (Word, 1990), p. 514.

8 Hans-Joachim Kraus, *Psalms 1–59* (Augsburg, 1988), p. 131.

9 Hans-Joachim Kraus, *Psalms 60–150* (Augsburg, 1989), p. 81.

10 Gerhard von Rad, *Theology of the Old Testament* (SCM, 1975), vol. 2, p. 374.

11 Ibid., p. 377.

12 A. B. Davidson, *Theology of the Old Testament* (T. & T. Clark, 1952), p. 374.

13 Paul R. Rabbe, *Obadiah*, Anchor Bible (Doubleday, 1996), p. 200.

14 John Watts, *Isaiah 1–33*, Word Biblical Commentary (Word, 1985), p. 35.

15 Otto J. Baab, *The Theology of the Old Testament* (Abingdon-Cokesbury, 1931), p. 213.

16 Tate, *Psalms 51–100*, p. 403.

3. THE FOUNDATIONS OF CHRISTIAN HOPE

1 William Dumbrell, *The Search for Order: Biblical Eschatology in Focus* (Baker, 1994), p. 187.

2 Herman Ridderbos, *The Coming of the Kingdom* (Presbyterian & Reformed, 1962), pp. 20–21.

3 Hans Conzelmann, *An Outline of the Theology of the New Testament* (SCM, 1969), p. 110.

4 Ridderbos, *Coming of the Kingdom*, p. 25.

5 Ibid., p. 36.

6 Albert Schweitzer, *The Mystery of the Kingdom of God* (Macmillan, 1950), p. 160.

7 Ibid., p. 168.

8 Albert Schweitzer, *The Quest for the Historical Jesus* (Macmillan, 1950), pp. 370–371.

9 Donald Hagner, *Matthew 1–13*, Word Biblical Commentary (Word, 1993), p. 279.

10 G. E. Ladd, *A Theology of the New Testament* (Lutterworth, 1974), p. 200.

11 Craig Evans, *Mark 8:27–16:20*, Word Biblical Commentary (Nelson, 2001), p. 28.

12 William Lane, *The Gospel of Mark*, New International Commentary of the New Testament (Eerdmans, 1974), p. 314.

13 Evans, *Mark 8:27–16:20*, p. 335.

14 Lane, *Gospel of Mark*, p. 458.

15 Ibid., p. 459.

16 Ridderbos, *Paul* (Eerdmans, 1975), p. 490.

17 Gordon Fee, *The First Epistle to the Corinthians*, New International Commentary on the New Testament (Eerdmans, 1987), p. 800. See also Hans Conzelmann, *1 Corinthians* (Fortress, 1975), p. 290.

18 Ridderbos, *Paul*, p. 491.

19 David Wenham, *Paul: Follower of Jesus or Founder of Christianity?* (Eerdmans, 1995), pp. 297–298.

20 James Dunn, *Romans 9–16*, Word Biblical Commentary (Word, 1988), p. 786.

21 F. F. Bruce, *1 & 2 Thessalonians*, Word Biblical Commentary (Word, 1982), p. 167.

22 Joseph Fitzmyer, *Romans*, Anchor Bible (Doubleday, 1993), p. 508.

23 Ibid., p. 508.

24 James Dunn, *Romans 1–8*, Word Biblical Commentary (Word, 1988), p. 487.

25 Ridderbos, *Paul*, p. 496.

26 Ladd, *Theology of the New Testament*, p. 551.

27 Hans Schwarz, *Eschatology* (Eerdmans, 2000), p. 96.

28 Ridderbos, *Paul*, p. 53.

4. THE LAST ENEMY

1 Wolfhart Pannenberg, 'Can Christianity Do Without An Eschatology?' *The Christian Hope*, SPCK Theological Collections (SPCK, 1970), p. 25.

2 Frena Bloomfield, *The Book of Chinese Beliefs* (Arrow, 1989), p. 36.

3 Benjamin Schwartz, *The World of Thought in Ancient China* (Harvard University Press, 1985), p. 254.

4 Theodosius Dobzhansky, *The Biology of Ultimate Concern* (New American Library, 1967), pp. 68–70.

5 Paul Helm, *The Last Things: Death, Judgement, Heaven and Hell* (Banner of Truth Trust, 1989), pp. 36–37.

6 Karl Jaspers, *The Way to Wisdom* (Yale University, 1951), p. 53.

7 Christopher A. Pallis, 'Death', *The New Encyclopedia Britannica*, 15th edn, vol. 16, p. 984.

8 Hans Schwarz, *Eschatology* (Eerdmans, 2000), p. 250.

9   Helmut Lehman (ed.), *Luther's Works* (Muhleanburg, 1959), vol. 51, p. 234.

10 Anthony Hoekema, *The Four Major Cults* (Eerdmans, 1963), p. 345.

11 W. D. Davies, *Paul and Rabbinic Judaism* (SPCK, 1955), pp. 317–318.

12 Millard Erickson, *Christian Theology* (Baker, 1985), p. 1182.

13 Wolfhart Pannenberg, *Systematic Theology* (Eerdmans, 1998), vol. 3, p. 571.

14 Ibid., p. 572.

15 Georges Florovsky, 'The "Immortality" of the Soul', *Collected Works*, pp. 111–112.

16 For a defence of disembodied existence, see Paul Helm, 'A Theory of Disembodied Survival and Re-embodied Existence', *Religious Studies* 14.1 (March 1978), pp. 15–26.

17 Schwarz, *Eschatology*, p. 286.

18 Ibid., p. 287.

19 G. E. Ladd, *The Last Things* (Eerdmans, 1978), p. 79.

20 Ibid., p. 78.

21 Gregory of Nyssa, 'On the Soul and the Resurrection', in Philip Schaff and Henry Wace (eds.), *Nicene and Post-Nicene Fathers of the Christian Church*, 2nd series (Eerdmans, 1954), vol. 5, p. 430.

22 Ibid., p. 446.

23 Schwarz, *Eschatology*, p. 290.

5. The coming of the Lord

1   Romano Guardini, *Eternal Life* (Sophia Institute Press, 1989), p. 105.

2   Helmut Thielicke, *The Evangelical Faith* (Eerdmans, 1982), vol. 3, p. 439.

3   Ralph Martin, *Is Jesus Coming Soon?* (Ignatius, 1983), p. 54.

4   See also 2 Corinthians 10:10.

5   G. E. Ladd, *The Last Things* (Eerdmans, 1978), p. 52.

6   Martin, *Is Jesus Coming Soon?* p. 56.

7   William Newton Clarke, *An Outline of Christian Theology* (Scribner, 1901), p. 444.

8   Wayne Grudem, *Systematic Theology* (IVP, 1994), p. 1092.

9   F. F. Bruce, *The Book of Acts*, New International Commentary on the New Testament (Eerdmans, 1983), p. 41.

10 Martin, *Is Jesus Coming Soon?* p. 57.

11 G. C. Berkouwer, *The Return of Christ* (Eerdmans, 1972), p. 141.

12 Philip Hughes, *A Commentary on the Epistle to the Hebrews* (Eerdmans, 1977), p. 389.

13 Louis Berkhof, *Systematic Theology* (Eerdmans, 1953), p. 706.

14 Martin, *Is Jesus Coming Soon?* p. 56.

15 Helmut Thielicke, *The Evangelical Faith* (Eerdmans, 1982), vol. 3, pp. 439–440.

16 Martin, *Is Jesus Coming Soon?* p. 97.

17 Guardini, *Eternal Life*, p. 95.

18 Berkhof, *Systematic Theology*, p. 731.

19 George Beasley-Murray, *John*, Word Biblical Commentary (Word, 1987), p. 218.

20 Stephen Travis, *I Believe in the Second Coming of Jesus* (Eerdmans, 1982), p. 195.

21 Ibid., p. 190.

22 Martin, *Is Jesus Coming Soon?* p. 104.

23 Stanley Samartha, *One Christ – Many Religions* (Orbis, 1991), p. 83.

24 Stanley Samartha, 'The Progress and Promise of the Inter-Religious Dialogues', *Journal of Ecumenical Studies* (1972), pp. 473–474.

25 See Roland Chia, *Revelation and Theology: The Knowledge of God According to Barth and Balthasar* (Peter Lang, 1999).

26 John Calvin, *The Epistles of Paul to the Romans and Thessalonians*, Calvin's New Testament Commentaries (Eerdmans, 1960), p. 29.

27 Ibid., p. 31.

28 James D. G. Dunn, *Romans 1–8*, Word Biblical Commentary (Word, 1988), p. 103.

6. THE PARTING OF WAYS

1   C. S. Lewis, *The Weight of Glory and Other Addresses* (Eerdmans, 1979), p. 3.

2   Ulrich Simon, *Heaven in Christian Tradition* (Harper, 1958), p. 237.

3   Millard Erickson, *The Christian Faith* (Baker, 1975), p. 1233.

4   Ibid., p. 1234.

5   See Matthew 5:16, 45; 6:1; 7:11; 18:14. Another variation is 'my Father who is in heaven'. See Matthew 7:21; 10:32, 33; 12:50; 16:17; 18:10, 19.

6   John F. Walvoord, *The Revelation of Jesus Christ* (Moody, 1966), p. 325.

7   Paul Helm, *The Last Things* (Banner of Truth Trust, 1989), p. 89.

8   John Calvin, *Galatians, Ephesians, Philippians and Colossians*, Calvin's New Testament Commentaries (Eerdmans, 1965), p. 143.

9   Philip Edgcumbe Hughes, *A Commentary on the Epistle to the Hebrews* (Eerdmans, 1977), p. 143.

10 Simon, *Heaven*, p. 234.

11 Ibid., p. 233.

12 See George Beasley-Murray, *John*, Word Biblical Commentary (Word, 1987), pp. 74–75.

13 Helm, *Last Things*, p. 94.

14 Simon, *Heaven*, p. 236.

15 Nels Ferré, *The Christian Understanding of God* (Harper, 1951), pp. 233–234.

16 William Crockett, 'The Metaphorical View', in William Crockett (ed.), *Four Views of Hell* (Zondervan, 1992), p. 55.

17 Clark Pinnock, 'The Conditional View', in ibid., p. 136.

18 Edward William Fudge and Robert A. Peterson, *Two Views of Hell: A Biblical and Theological Dialogue* (IVP, 2000).

19 Edward William Fudge, *The Fire That Consumes: The Biblical Case for Conditional Immortality* (Paternoster, 1994).

20 Robert A. Peterson, *Hell on Trial: The Case for Eternal Punishment* (Presbyterian & Reformed, 1995).

21 Pinnock, 'Conditional View', p. 135.

22 Ibid., p. 140.

23 Ibid.

24 Ibid., p. 144.

25 Ibid., p. 146.

26 Ibid., pp. 146–147.

27 David Edwards and John Stott, *Essentials: A Liberal–Evangelical Dialogue* (Hodder & Stoughton, 1988), p. 320.

28 Pinnock, 'Conditional View', p. 148.

29 Ibid., p. 151.

30 Ibid., p. 152.

31 See John Walvoord, 'The Literal View', in Crockett, *Four Views on Hell*, pp. 11–28.

32 Crockett, 'Metaphorical View', p. 59.

33 Quoted in John A. T. Robinson, *In the End God* (Harper & Row, 1968), p. 131, n. 8.

34 Augustine, *City of God*, translated by Henry Bettenson (Penguin, 1972), 21.23.

35 Ibid., 12.

36 Thomas Aquinas, *Summa Theologiae* (Christian Classics, 1981), 1a2ae.87.A.

37 Pinnock, 'Conditional View', p. 154.

38 Edwards and Stott, *Essentials*, p. 107.

39 Helm, *Last Things*, pp. 116–117.

40 Ibid.

7. A NEW WORLD COMING

1 G. E. Ladd, *The Presence of the Future* (Eerdmans, 1974), p. 326.

2 Bruce Milne, *I Want to Know What the Bible Says About the End of the World* (Kingsway, 1979), pp. 44–45.

3 Ladd, *Presence of the Future*, pp. 326–327 (italics original).

4 John Stott, *The Message of Thessalonians*, Bible Speaks Today (IVP, 1991), p. 158.

5 John Calvin, *The Epistles of Paul to the Romans and Thessalonians*, Calvin's New Testament Commentaries (Eerdmans, 1973), p. 401.

6 G. E. Ladd, *The Last Things* (Eerdmans, 1978), p. 63.

7 Milne, *End of the World*, p. 68.

8 G. E. Ladd, 'Historic Premillennialism', in Robert G. Clouse (ed.), *The Meaning of the Millennium: Four Views* (IVP, 1977), p. 17.

9 Ibid., pp. 17–18.

10 G. E. Ladd, *Central Questions About the Kingdom of God* (Eerdmans, 1952), p. 141.

11 Justin Martyr, *Dialogue with Trypho, A Jew*, in A. Roberts and J. Donaldson (eds.), *The Ante-Nicene Fathers: Translation of the Fathers Down to A.D. 325* (Eerdmans, 1975), vol. 1, p. 239.

12 Irenaeus, *Against Heresies* 5.33; Roberts and Donaldson, *Ante-Nicene Fathers*, vol. 1, p. 563.

13 Grenz, *Millennial Maze* (IVP, 1992), p. 140.

14 Archibald Hughes, *A New Heaven and New Earth* (Marshall, Morgan & Scott, 1958), pp. 83–105.

15 Anthony Hoekema, 'Historic Premillennialism: An Amillennial Response', in Clouse, *Meaning of the Millennium*, p. 59.

16 Loraine Boettner, *The Millennium* (Presbyterian & Reformed, 1957), p. 4.

17 Jürgen Moltmann, *The Coming of God* (Fortress, 1996), p. 154.

18 Augustus Hopkins Strong, *Systematic Theology* (Griffith & Rowland, 1909), vol. 3, p. 108.

19 Grenz, *Millennial Maze*, p. 87.

20 Ibid., p. 86.

21 Berkhof, *Systematic Theology*, p. 708.

22 Grenz, *Millennial Maze*, p. 157.

23 Anthony Hoekema, *The Bible and the Future* (Paternoster, 1979), p. 227.

24 Anthony Hoekema, 'Amillennialism', in Clouse, *Meaning of the Millennium*, p. 164.

25 C. Ryrie, *Dispensationalism Today* (Moody, 1965), pp. 87–88.

26 John Walvoord, 'Interpreting Prophecy Today', *Bibliotheca Sacra* 139.533–556 (1982), pp. 3–12, 111–128, 205–215, 302–311.

27 Milne, *End of the World*, p. 87.

28 Grenz, *Millennial Maze*, p. 95.

29 Milne, *End of the World*, pp. 89–90.

30 Grenz, *Millennial Maze*, p. 109.

31 Hoekema, *Bible and the Future*, p. 167.

32 Ibid.

33 See G. E. Ladd, *The Blessed Hope* (Eerdmans, 1956), p. 144.

34 Milne, *End of the World*, p. 91.

35 Dermot Lane, *Keeping Hope Alive: Stirrings in Christian Theology* (Gill & Macmillan, 1996), p. 188.

36 Ryrie, *Dispensationalism Today*, p. 158.

37 Jürgen Moltmann, *The Coming of God* (Fortress, 2000), p. 269.

38 Robert Mounce, *The Book of Revelation*, New International Commentary of the New Testament (Eerdmans, 1977), p. 373.

39 Hoekema, *Bible and the Future*, p. 283.

40 Hans Schwarz, *Eschatology* (Eerdmans, 2000), p. 397.

41 Mounce, *Revelation*, p. 372.

8. Living in Hope

1   Glenn Tinder, *The Fabric of Hope* (Scholars Press, 1999), p. 43.

2   Emil Brunner, *Eternal Hope* (Lutterworth, 1954), p. 28.

3   Joseph Ratzinger, *To Look on Christ* (St Paul, 1978), p. 61.

4   James D. G. Dunn, *Romans 1–8*, Word Biblical Commentary (Word, 1988), p. 475.

5   Erik Strand, 'Worship as a Sign of the End', in William H. Lazareth (ed.), *Hope for the Future: Theological Voices in the Pastorate* (Eerdmans, 2002), p. 176.

6   David Henderson, 'The Eschatological and Doxological Character of the Church in the World', in Lazareth, *Hope for the Future*, p. 169.

7   Tinder, *Fabric of Hope*, p. 84.

8   James White, *Introduction to Christian Worship*, 3rd edn (Abingdon, 2000), pp. 217ff.

9   Geoffrey Wainwright, *Eucharist and Eschatology* (Epworth, 1971), p. 2.

10 Ibid., p. 58.

11 Rebecca Kuiken, 'Hopeful Feasting: Eucharist and Eschatology', in Lazareth, *Hope for the Future*, p. 197.

12 Michael Buckley, *At the Origins of Atheism* (Yale University Press, 1987).

13 Kenneth Surin, *Theology and the Problem of Evil* (Blackwell, 1986).

14 Terrence Tilley, *The Evils of Theodicy* (Wipf & Stock, 2000).

15 Surin, *Theology and the Problem of Evil*, p. 9.

16 Henri Blocher, *Evil and the Cross* (Apollos, 1990), p. 128.

17 Colin Gunton, *The Triune Creator* (T. & T. Clark, 1998), p. 172.

18 Tinder, *Fabric of Hope*, p. 70.

19 Bantam, 1970.

20 Pannenberg, *Systematic Theology*, vol. 3, p. 634.

21 Ibid., p. 637.

22 Gunton, *Triune Creator*, p. 173.

23 Blocher, *Evil and the Cross*, p. 132.

24 Pannenberg, *Systematic Theology*, vol. 3, p. 642.

25 Kazoh Kitamori, *Theology of the Pain of God* (John Knox, 1958), p. 144.

26 Ian Ker, *John Henry Newman: A Biography* (Oxford University Press, 1988), pp. 79–80.

27 Tinder, *Fabric of Hope*, p. 56.

28 Ibid., p. 63.

29 Richard Bauckham and Trevor Hart, *Hope Against Hope: Christian Eschatology at the Turn of the Millennium* (Eerdmans, 1999), p. 207.